Advocacy and Public Speaking

Advocacy and Public Speaking:

A Student's Introduction

Derek Halbert and Hayley Whitaker
University of Chester Law School, 2016

With a Foreword by
**The Rt Hon. the Lord Thomas
of Cwmgiedd Kt, PC**
Lord Chief Justice of England and Wales

University of Chester Press

First published 2016
by University of Chester Press
Parkgate Road
Chester CH1 4BJ

Printed and bound in the UK by the
LIS Print Unit
University of Chester
Cover designed by the LIS Graphics Team
University of Chester

A catalogue record of this book is available
from the British Library

ISBN 978-1-908258-27-4

To Heather
to whom I owe
almost everything
DRH

To Mum and Nanna
who always encouraged
me to persevere
HW

CONTENTS

Contents

FOREWORD

This book has a two-fold purpose – to provide an introduction to public speaking and to explain the basic skills needed for the specialised profession of advocacy. Public speaking is an essential skill everyone should learn. Simple, though the rules may be, this short book spells them out with great clarity. It enlivens them by what some would call well-known 'one-liners' that introduce each rule. In fact these 'one-liners' are pithily expressed phrases that also serve to underline the fact that advocacy is one of the oldest professions. Indeed some of the techniques developed by Marcus Tullius Cicero, the greatest orator in the history of ancient Rome who deployed his art at times to great effect in speeches in criminal cases, still present some useful pointers.

The book then turns to its second purpose by building on this first part to provide a concise guide to advocacy. When I was called to the bar, many, many years ago, the concept of advocacy tuition was non-existent; in fact, to suggest such a thing might have been considered heretical. You learnt by watching others in times when there was little work and from your mistakes.

The teaching of advocacy, in one way or another, is now a welcome common feature of university, law school, professional training, and onward career development. From my perspective, this is of greatest benefit to judges and litigants, as the interests of justice require the highest professional standards of advocates when they appear in court.

Advocacy and Public Speaking

Most judges will have their own view as to what makes a successful advocate. My personal view is that what is required is mastery of the subject on which the advocate is to argue through hard work and preparation, the observance of the highest ethical standards and the skilful deployment of the advocate's arts of persuasion. Each of these three is carefully explained in this book.

It is, in short, an indispensable companion to any student aspiring to the highest standards of advocacy. It contains very practical advice as to various tasks the advocate has to perform and the standards to which the advocate must adhere. It is easy to follow and, more importantly, to apply. It is structured so that one can 'dip in', as necessary, once the reader has absorbed the overall approach.

So, to the aspirant advocate or those seeking to develop their craft: read on. Then, keeping the theory in mind, consider the annexes or the online examples; visit courts to observe real cases; or read the transcripts of some of history's greatest trials. You can then reflect on and seek to emulate the great advocates. Lastly, and most importantly, practise. Do not be disheartened by the bumps along the way. And take courage from the fact that refining the art of advocacy really does take time and the very best advocates continually seek to do so.

The Rt Hon. The Lord Thomas of Cwmgiedd,
Lord Chief Justice of England and Wales
March 2016

PREFACE

This book is intended to assist students whose career pathway will involve advocacy or oratory. There is, of course, a fundamental difference between the two. Oratory involves speaking in public in whatever context. A professional advocate's public speaking will normally be confined to the courtroom or tribunal but he or she must have a much wider skill set, of which oratory is one element.

Most of those who read this book will be law students but it is hoped that Chapters 1 and 2 and the Appendix may be of help to any student who expects to have to speak in front of an audience.

Much of what this book has to say about public speaking could be derived from common sense. But, perhaps because of the pressure felt by those who need to speak in public, many speakers either forget the rules or are unable to follow them.

Many of the greatest speeches of the last hundred years or so have been recorded either as audio or video. Some of the great speeches made before sound recording was invented have been performed by actors in films or otherwise recorded. Much of this material is readily available on the Internet. There are many references to it in the text. If possible, read Chapters 1 and 2 of this book while sitting in front of a computer with Internet access so that you can watch and listen to the recordings while reading.

Many more of the great speeches of pre-recording times are available as text. These too repay study. The text of a few of the great speeches will be found in the Appendix with annotations highlighting the rhetorical devices used by the speakers.

Chapters 3 to 10 of this work are aimed specifically at students who wish to become advocates, whether as solicitors or as barristers. Chapters 3 to 9 are intended to provide an introduction to the techniques of advocacy required by professional advocates and they are intended for students both at university level and when studying on one of the professional training courses.

Chapter 10 gives some suggestions on how the techniques taught by this book can be used to enhance the chances of success in applications for pupillage, training contracts or other positions within the legal profession as a whole.

Mark Twain once wrote *'The secret of getting ahead is getting started.'*

So – read on!

ABOUT THE AUTHORS

His Honour Derek Halbert, MA (Cantab), BA (Open), LLD (Chester) was for 24 years a member of the bar in Chester and then for 20 years a Circuit Judge until his retirement in September 2015. He is now an Honorary Senior Lecturer in Law at the University of Chester.

Hayley Whitaker, LLB (Chester), MA (Chester) is a member of the bar of England and Wales and a Lecturer in Law at the University of Chester where she is in the process of preparing her doctoral thesis. She is also responsible for the University's course on Public Speaking and Advocacy.

ABBREVIATIONS

ADR – Alternative Dispute Resolution

BCOC – Bar Standards Board Code of Conduct

BSB – Bar Standards Board

CJ – Chief Justice

CPR – Civil Procedure Rules

CV – Curriculum vitae

ER – English Reports

FPR – Family Procedure Rules

HH – His Honour

HTML – Hypertext markup language

KISS – Keep it short and simple

LCJ – Lord Chief Justice

MDF – Medium density fibreboard

MIAM – Family Mediation Information and Assessment Meeting

MedLR – Medical Law Reports

MR – Master of the Rolls

Abbreviations

P – President (of the Family Division)

PD – Practice Direction

PDF – Portable document format

QAA – Quality Assurance Agency for Higher Education

SCOC – The Law Society Solicitors' Code of Conduct

SRA – Solicitors Regulation Authority

QC – Queen's Counsel

VRD – Volunteer Reserve Decoration (Royal Navy)

Please Note that in Chapter 4, section 3, there is an explanation of case references which translates many of the acronyms and abbreviations used in referring to law reports. Also, in Chapter 4, section 6, there is an explanation of how to address and how to refer to judges both orally and in writing which deals with many of the acronyms and abbreviations of that subject. As a result, the acronyms and abbreviations included in those sections are not reproduced here unless they appear elsewhere in the text of this book.

CHAPTER 1

TWELVE RULES FOR SPEAKING IN PUBLIC

*Or what so pleasing to the understanding and the ear as
a speech adorned and polished with wise reflections
and dignified language?*
Marcus Tullius Cicero – *De Oratore*, Vol. 8 para 31

The art of Oratory (Rhetoric) is extremely ancient.
Confucius (551–479 BC) wrote disparagingly of orators
and there is an extensive treatise on the subject by
Aristotle (384–322 BC), who was a tutor to Alexander
the Great and who defined Rhetoric as:

*'the power to observe the persuasiveness of which any
particular matter admits'*.

That definition is as accurate today as it was when it
was written. Moreover, the art has changed very little
over the millennia of its existence, despite the changes
both in the nature of civilisation and in the languages
used. A good translation of Aristotle's Treatise, ***The Art
of Rhetoric*** is available as a Penguin Classic.

Marcus Tullius Cicero (106–43 BC), who is widely
regarded as having been one of the greatest advocates
and orators in history, wrote two works on orators and
one on Rhetoric. They are all available with both the
original Latin text and an English translation in the
'Loeb Classical Library' series published by Harvard
University Press.

Advocacy and Public Speaking

In Book 1 of *Rhetorica Ad C. Herennium (De Ratione Dicendi)* [*To Gaius Herennius (On the Theory of Public Speaking)*], Cicero identified five techniques (he used the Latin word *res* which means things), which he said should be applied by an orator:

(1) **Inventio:** (Invention)
Research and assemble the material for the speech you wish to present.
(2) **Dispositio:** (Arrangement)
Assemble the sections of the argument in a logical order.
(3) **Elocutio:** (Elocution/style)
Make use of the devices of rhetoric.
(4) **Memoria:** (Memory)
Memorise your speech so that you can deliver it without looking constantly at your notes.
(5) **Pronuntiatio:** (Delivery)
Use gestures, facial expressions and modulation of the voice, etc.

These, he said, can be acquired by **Arte** (Theory), **Imitatione** (Imitation) and **Exercitatione** (Practice).

A little later, in *De Oratore*, Cicero added a sixth technique:

(6) **Decorum:** (Appropriateness)
Use language suitable to the occasion and the audience.

Twelve Rules for Speaking in Public

These elements of skill in public speaking and the three methods required to learn them are still as relevant today as they were when written.

Many attempts have been made to list the 'ten best speeches of all time'. The selection process is an entirely subjective one; the criteria differ and, of course, so do the results. Many orators have made outstanding or memorable speeches but few obtain more than one citation in any such list. The two who do so are Winston Churchill and John F Kennedy. They are both quoted frequently in this book.

As Cicero said, there are three processes essential to learning oratory:

(1) Learn the rules of oratory and the skills of rhetoric. Read the rest of this chapter and read Cicero and Aristotle.

(2) Study the great speeches throughout history and learn to identify and copy the techniques employed by the great speakers. Do not confine yourself to the material used as examples in this book. Many more are available online. All you need do is use a search engine and enter the name of the orator and either a key word or phrase from the speech or a reference to the occasion. If you simply search for 'great speeches' you will find many lists. If possible, choose a video recording; if video is not available, listen to a sound recording. Where all you can do is read the text, do so.

(3) Practise. Take on as much public speaking as you reasonably can. Take part in university moots. Join the debating society. Take every opportunity to get used to speaking in front of an audience. Recite your speeches to friends or family and get them to tell you what they think you should do differently. Speak to a mirror. Best of all, practise in front of a video camera and then watch the playback. You will be very surprised at how much useful self-criticism you are able to perform. Those who now teach the Bar Professional Training Course and the Legal Practice Course make extensive use of this technique.

The rest of this chapter sets out the authors' formulation of twelve rules for public speakers. Most of them are reflected in what Cicero wrote, although they are more numerous than Cicero's canons and rather more specific.

If you can ever speak half as well as the men and women whose speeches are considered in this chapter, your future prospects will be significantly improved.

Twelve Rules for Speaking in Public

Rule 1: Prepare Thoroughly

Before anything else, preparation is the key to success.
Alexander Graham Bell

In the early 1970s, the Head of the barristers' chambers at 39 Whitefriars, Chester, David Lloyd-Jones VRD (later HH Judge) would tell new pupils: '*You succeed in this profession by meticulous attention to detail.*' He was unquestionably correct. There is no substitute for thorough preparation.

If you are to present a legal argument you must know and understand it. If you cite authorities in support of it, it is essential that you have read them. Then if any member of the audience or the tribunal you are attempting to convince asks for any peripheral detail, you will be able to answer.

If you are addressing a lecture audience, again you may be asked for clarification or further detail. It is vital that you can produce an intelligent response.

Although this rule is very simple to state, it is by far the most important of all. No matter how good your rhetorical skills, you will not be an effective advocate or orator if you do not have a very thorough knowledge of your subject matter.

A very amusing illustration of just how badly things can go wrong for a speaker who has not prepared adequately is John Cleese's attempt at anti-Roman rabble-rousing in the Monty Python film *The Life of*

Brian (the clip is available online). The speaker asks (intending the question to be rhetorical): *'What have the Romans ever done for us?'* He sits back expecting silence but instead the audience respond with a list of the benefits of Roman occupation, beginning with the aqueduct. He tries again *'Apart from* [the items in the list] *what have the Romans ever done for us?'* But again the audience respond with more items for the list.

This is a fictitious but very effective example. Imagine you were advancing a legal argument in the Court of Appeal and their Lordships could pick holes in your argument and identify flaws you had failed to anticipate just as easily as the audience addressed in this sketch. Not only would you inevitably lose the case, you would lose any reputation you had ever had as an advocate.

Rule 2: Speak Slowly and Clearly

'However,' said Dumbledore, speaking very slowly and clearly so that none of them could miss a word ...
J K Rowling, *Harry Potter and the Chamber of Secrets*

Before you read any more about this rule, go online and listen to the following speeches:

(1) Winston Churchill's speech to the House of Commons on 18 June 1940, which contains the phrase 'This was their finest hour'. A sound recording of the speech is available online.

(2) President John F Kennedy's inaugural address delivered on 20 January 1961. Several video recordings of the speech are readily available online. It is best to find one of the full speech, which was about 13 minutes long. The full text, together with comments on the rhetorical devices used is in the Appendix to this volume.

The two speeches you have just heard are in many ways very different. Churchill's was delivered with much less variation in tone and at moderate volume. There was less emotion in his voice because he was addressing the House of Commons rather than a mass audience.

Conversely, John F Kennedy's speech was delivered at relatively high volume and with much more emotion in his tone and his choice of words.

However, despite these differences, they have in common that both men spoke slowly and very clearly. Churchill maintained a fairly even pace throughout while John F Kennedy increased his pace a little from time to time.

The rhythm of a speech is important. The phrases of both men were carefully measured and delivered with an almost musical attention to the meter.

There was very little risk that any member of either audience could mishear or misunderstand what had been said.

Rule 3: Talk to Your Audience, Not at Them

He speaks to me as if I were a public meeting.
Queen Victoria
[of one of her Prime Ministers, William E Gladstone]

This is one aspect of what Cicero called 'Decorum', which can best be translated in this context as 'appropriateness' or 'suitability'.

Most public speeches are intended to persuade. The advocate presenting a legal argument wishes to persuade the court that his or her legal argument is correct and that his or her interpretation of the law should be adopted. The same advocate presenting a speech to a jury in a criminal trial is trying to persuade them either to convict or acquit the defendant. The politician at the hustings is trying to persuade the electorate to vote for him or her.

In every one of these cases it is essential to establish proper communication with the audience. The techniques required are however different.

In presenting a legal argument there is little scope for rhetoric or emotion. What is required is a sound legal argument well supported by authority and that will have been created at the preparation stage. Presenting a legal argument is a highly specialised form of public speaking and its preparation is very detailed. Chapter 4 is specifically devoted to it.

Advocacy and Public Speaking

In almost all other public speaking contexts it is important to try to establish a rapport with the audience and, if possible, a sense of common purpose. It is important to be inclusive. **Inclusive language** is an important rhetorical device. Try to use sentences which refer to '*we*' because to do so creates a sense of communality. If you refer to the opposition as '*them*' or '*they*' it has the same effect. Try to keep the use of '*I*' and '*you*' to circumstances where you need to make a distinction between you and the audience.

Look at the text of John F Kennedy's inauguration speech in the Appendix. In the first ten paragraphs, '*we*', '*our*' or '*us*' appear 28 times but '*I*' appears only once.

Another very good example is another Churchill speech. This was delivered, also to the House of Commons, on 4 June 1940 and it is usually referred to as the 'We Shall Fight' speech. Go online and listen to it. The part everyone remembers is:

'*We shall fight in France. We shall fight on the seas and oceans. We shall fight with growing confidence and with growing strength in the air. We shall defend our island, whatever the cost may be. We shall fight on the beaches. We shall fight on the landing grounds. We shall fight in the fields and in the streets. We shall fight in the hills. We shall never surrender.*'

That quotation consists of nine consecutive sentences beginning '*We*'. The speech also makes numerous references to *'our'*, *'our island'* and *'our empire'*. It also uses a very powerful rhetorical technique, the **repeated key phrase** (see Rule 12).

Select the rest of your language for the same effect. Use simple language and phrases which will have a resonance for your audience.

The language a professional advocate is permitted to use to a jury is heavily restricted. It is utterly forbidden to express your own views or feelings. You may say *'I suggest'* or *'I submit'*. You may not say *'I think'* or *'I believe'*. Despite that restriction it is still possible to construct sentences which are inclusive. For example:

'Members of the jury, we are all men and women of the world. We all have memories of walking up to somebody on the street thinking we recognise them and then realising at the last minute, perhaps even after we have greeted them, that it isn't Fred after all. We have made a mistaken identification even of someone we thought we knew, even at close range and even in broad daylight. If you remember this and if you use your common sense and your knowledge of how the real world works, how can you possibly be sure that the purported identification of my client by David Bloggs is correct?'

This obeys all the rules but it is inclusive. It uses *'you'* only when this is essential. It establishes common ground by drawing on shared experience. It also ends with a **rhetorical question** (see Rule 12).

Maintain eye contact (we will return to this requirement later for other reasons). It is much easier to do so when addressing a single judge court than with a multiple judge court, a jury or a mass audience. Nevertheless, even with a large audience, look at them while you speak. If you do not, you will be talking at them not to them and this is much less effective.

This is one of the reasons why Cicero said a speech should be memorised because if you are reading it you cannot look at the audience.

One of the reasons for the popularity of the autocue is that it enables the speaker to keep his or her head up and face the audience and still read the notes of the speech.

Rule 4: Eliminate Nonsense Words

*An interjection ... is not a part of speech ... it is a noisy
utterance like the cry of an animal.*
F J Rahtz, *Higher English*

DO NOT interject words such as *'like'* or phrases such
as *'if you see what I mean'*, *'as I say'* or *'you know'*, in
circumstances where they are redundant or
meaningless. These words and phrases are common in
normal everyday speech, though potential orators or
advocates who use them a lot would be well advised to
ask their friends and family to help them to stop doing
it.

You may use *'like'* when you mean *'the same as'* or
'similar to' or as a verb when you mean *'have an affection
for'*. You may use *'Do you know?'* or *'Do you see what I
mean?'* when you are genuinely asking a question. Not
otherwise.

As an exercise, try Winston Churchill's speech,
delivered to the House of Commons on 20 August 1940,
which contains the sentence: *'Never in the field of human
conflict has so much been owed by so many to so few.'*

The text of the most important section is as follows:

*'The gratitude of every home in our island, in our empire and
indeed throughout the world, except in the abodes of the
guilty, goes out to the British airmen who, undaunted by
odds, unwearied in their constant challenge and mortal
danger, are turning the tide of the World War by their*

prowess and by their devotion. Never in the field of human conflict was so much owed by so many to so few.'

Stand in front of a mirror or a video camera and read it out loud. Or preferably memorise it and speak without needing to read. Try to speak as slowly as Churchill did and with pauses to lend extra meaning to the words, as he did.

Having done so, now try reciting it to the same mirror or camera but intersperse it with *'like'*, *'you know'* and *'do you see what I mean'*. Wherever you put the extra words you will immediately appreciate that the additional words destroy the impact of the language.

Rule 5: Make Use of Silence

*The right word may be effective, but no word was
ever as effective as a rightly timed pause.*
Mark Twain

Let thy speech be better than silence, or be silent.
Dionysius of Halicarnassus

The periods of time between phrases, sentences or
paragraphs in a speech are not merely gaps. They are,
or should be, tools in themselves and they should be
used as such.

Try the Churchill 'Never in the field ...' speech again.
Repeat the next paragraph aloud with pauses of about
half a second where the dashes appear.

*'Never – in the field of human conflict – has so much –
been owed by so many – to so few.'*

It sounds as good or perhaps even better with the
pauses. They give emphasis to the subject matter.

DO NOT make the sound 'erm'. A pause lends
emphasis; an 'erm' does not. It sounds indecisive and
uncertain.

If you reach a point where you cannot find the next
word, do not 'erm'; stop speaking altogether until you
have found the word you need.

An outstanding example of this technique was a speech
made at Indianapolis on 4 April 1968 by Robert

Kennedy, younger brother of John F Kennedy in which he announced the death of Martin Luther King (a video recording is readily available online and the text, with comments, is in the Appendix).

Robert Kennedy had written notes for the speech on the back of an envelope on the journey to Indianapolis. It can be seen in his hands in the video recording but he delivered the entire speech without looking at it.

The address lasted approximately five minutes but he uttered the sound 'erm' only once (within the first few seconds). On many other occasions he was clearly trying to think what word to use next but he simply paused, often for quite a long time. At one point he quoted Aeschylus who he said was his favourite poet. It took him a little time to recall the quotation in full but while he focused his memory, he made no attempt to fill the silence. The result was that when he did utter the quotation it had even more impact.

Sometimes it is feasible not merely to pause, but to remain totally silent for an extended period, particularly if you have achieved a reaction from your audience and are waiting for the applause or laughter to die down, or are waiting for a complex message to sink in.

A very good example is the part of **Gerard Hoffnung's** speech to the Oxford Union in 1958 which is usually subtitled **'The Bricklayer's Lament'**. A sound recording of the extract is available online. Listen to it.

Note three things: first, early in the extract, he used the word 'see?' It was not a meaningless interjection; he was asking the audience a question and it resulted in laughter, which was what he was trying to achieve. This illustrates that expressions such as 'see?' and 'do you see?' are perfectly usable when they have meaning.

Second, early in the speech he used small pauses between phrases. 'Erm' was not used at all.

Third, later in the speech, when he achieved a reaction from his audience, he was prepared to wait quite long periods of time in silence. It was particularly effective in this speech because one of the things that makes the story so funny is that you can work out what is going to happen next, and as his audience began to do this, he paused to let them do it, which made them laugh. He then delivered the line which they were expecting to hear and they laughed again. Bear in mind that what he was trying to do was to make the audience laugh.

Humour was the only purpose of this speech and by pausing appropriately he achieved twice as much laughter from the audience.

This extract from the speech lasts about six and a half minutes. If it had been spoken without the pauses it would have lasted less than three. More than half the time, the speaker was silent. Do not make the mistake of being uncomfortable with silence or feeling that it is necessary to fill the silence with something or to speak continuously. Silence is a useful tool. Use it appropriately.

'The Bricklayer's Lament' was only part of a much longer speech, but posterity remembers the bricklayer much more than the rest of the speech, possibly because the remainder of the speech was delivered less well.

Rule 6: Try to Think in Complete Sentences

*Over the years, I've trained myself to speak using the
same language I would use if I were typing: meaning
using full sentences in the way that paragraphs
and scenes are arranged.*
Kevin J Anderson

If you have composed a speech in its entirety in
advance and memorised it to perfection, this rule will
have little application but in normal circumstances
when the speaker knows what he intends to say but has
not planned down to the last word, it will be necessary
for him or her to decide precisely what words to use as
he or she proceeds. This is another reason for speaking
slowly. To do so will give you more time to compose
each phrase before uttering it.

However, if you compose only phrases, sooner or later
you will come to a point where you have started a
sentence and cannot work out how to end it. You will
then be forced to a choice between a clumsy ending,
starting again or leaving the sentence unfinished. None
of those will satisfy the audience. The impression you
give will be one of indecision or uncertainty.

The problem will be much reduced if you learn to think
in complete sentences and to formulate, before you
speak, not only each phrase but each sentence.

It will be easier to do this if you keep your sentences
short and simple, which is one of the principles of
rhetoric (see Rule 12) but, simple or complex, if you

learn always to compose a complete sentence before you begin to speak, the problem will not arise.

You may need to pause between sentences to enable you to do it but it has already been demonstrated that this is beneficial rather than harmful.

Another common error which can be avoided by thinking in complete sentences is a tendency to be sidetracked in the middle of one sentence, into starting another. The usual result of doing this is that the original sentence is never completed, which ruins both the flow of the speech and the ability of the audience to understand what is being said.

Rule 7: Use Appropriate Language

*If you talk to a man in a language he understands,
that goes to his head. If you talk to him in his
language, that goes to his heart.*
Nelson Mandela

This is an aspect of what Cicero called 'Decorum'. Aristotle also wrote about it in his book **'Rhetoric'**, in which he said that language should correspond to its subject and that aptness of language tends to make people believe what the speaker is saying.

Adjust the language you use so that it is suitable for your subject and your audience. This applies both to the complexity of the vocabulary you use and to the emotional content of the words.

As to complexity of language, to refer to '*The genesis and metamorphosis of the project*' might work at a scientific symposium or perhaps in the Court of Appeal but it would not go down so well if you were addressing a union meeting on a building site. '*The way this system started and the way it has changed since*' would be a lot better.

As to words with a high emotional content, '*I implore you to consider with great care whether this case is proved to the required standard*' would be acceptable in addressing a jury. To 'implore' the Court of Appeal would be regarded as excessively flowery language and would probably raise eyebrows, if not worse.

Advocacy and Public Speaking

It is important to use language which will strike a chord with your audience. In most cases this will involve changing the vocabulary or the complexity of the sentences you use to suit the audience. However, in some cases it can add great emphasis to what you say if you change language altogether.

A very good example was the speech of John F Kennedy in Berlin in 1963 in which he twice used the phrase *'Ich bin ein Berliner'* (a video recording is available online).

In this speech, John F Kennedy made use of a rhetorical technique which we call the **'repeated key phrase'** (see Rule 12 below). He made several references to those who, for various reasons, had said there was any merit in the Communist system, ending each reference with the expression *'Let them come to Berlin.'* However, on the last occasion he used the phrase he spoke in German. This struck a chord with his audience and they responded with very loud applause. He used the same technique at the beginning of the address when he drew a parallel between *'Civis Romanus sum'* and *'Ich bin ein Berliner'* which he repeated at the end of the speech.

Those who have a command of German will have noticed that John F Kennedy should not have said *'Ich bin **ein** Berliner'* but *'Ich bin Berliner'* (This is yet another pointer to the need for thorough preparation. He clearly did not speak German well himself so he, or perhaps his speech writers, should have checked the line with someone who was fluent before he used it). Despite this, it was clear from the audience reaction that the rhetorical device worked.

Take great care in the selection of appropriate language. Except in quotations it is very seldom appropriate to use slang and it is never appropriate to swear. You should not use language too complex or too technical for your audience but neither should you over simplify or 'talk down' to them. If you do, you will sound patronising.

Rule 8: Use Appropriate Body Language

*The secret of success is sincerity. Once you can
fake that you've got it made.*
Jean Giraudoux

This is part of what Cicero referred to as 'Actio', i.e. delivery. You should use both facial expression and body movement to give an impression of sincerity and to add emphasis to what you say. If you appear sincere, particularly when addressing a jury, you will have more impact than otherwise.

First, adopt a stance facing your audience with your feet slightly apart and your weight evenly distributed and stand upright. This will give you an appearance of confidence and authority.

Next, as far as possible, keep your eyes on the person or people you are talking to. We have already referred to this in the context of talking to rather than at the audience, but eye contact is important for other reasons. It is a widely recognised body language symbol in Western Europe and North America that if the speaker does not meet the eyes of the person addressed, he may well not be telling the truth.

For this reason, although it is perfectly legitimate to write out a speech in full in advance, indeed, it is often a very good idea, NEVER deliver the speech by reading it (Cicero covered this under the heading Memoria).

Twelve Rules for Speaking in Public

If you just read your notes you will look down continuously and not look at the audience. It will also be difficult to stand upright. You will tend to stoop forward.

It matters less when addressing a very large audience from a stage or a pulpit, but it still matters. It is less important when addressing a legal argument to a judge than when delivering a closing speech to a jury, but on all occasions it still matters.

You should also be aware that body language varies in different cultures. South Asian people do not meet the eye of the person to whom they are speaking because to do so is considered disrespectful. If you ever have to make a speech outside a European or North American context, you would do well to check on the body language customs of the relevant country.

Other body language such as arm and hand movements can lend great emphasis to words. Almost all politicians use them because they are told to by PR consultants.

If you watch a video recording of John F Kennedy's speech in Berlin you will see that he used his hands and arms extensively. When he made a particularly forceful point he banged his fist on the lectern. His face was very animated and he smiled a great deal.

However, unless you have acting skills or training, do not use excess or artificial arm and hand movements:

let them come naturally with the words you use. An artificial and excessive use of such gestures is far worse than none at all.

In addition, as with your choice of language, make sure your gestures are appropriate to the occasion and to the audience. Hand and arm gestures are very useful in making a political speech to a mass audience. Only very restrained use of the hands would be appropriate in advancing a legal argument. You might use a pointed finger when addressing a jury but it would not be appropriate when addressing the Court of Appeal.

Other video/film recordings of John F Kennedy's speeches show him making extensive use of hand gestures, even when he was addressing a mass audience, few of whom could see him clearly.

Video/film recordings of Churchill speaking are rather more rare, but extracts from several can be found online. His speech to the American Congress in January 1942 shows that he too made good use both of his hands and also sometimes emphasised what he was saying by nodding his head.

Rule 9: Look at the Reaction of Your Audience

*The face is a picture of the mind with the eyes
as its interpreter.*
Marcus Tullius Cicero

You need to observe the progress of your efforts. If, for example, you are addressing a jury, you need to know whether what you are saying is achieving the desired effect or not and you will usually be able to read this in the expressions on their faces.

Even when you are not directly addressing the audience, for example when you are examining or cross-examining a witness, although obviously you need to make eye contact with the witness most of the time, you still need to look at the audience (the judge or the jury) just briefly at least every so often in order to check that you are still achieving what you want.

Some years ago a driver was prosecuted for causing death by dangerous driving. He had been involved in an accident with another vehicle driven by a man of limited intelligence who had been killed in the impact. The nature of the defence required some blame to be placed on the driving of this man.

The advocate responsible for the defence chose to do this by cross-examining the man's mother (who had not been present at the accident and would not normally have been called to give oral evidence at all) about his low intelligence. The first question was to this effect. As he asked it, he was looking down at his notes.

If he had seen the terrible distress of the mother or the facial expressions of the jury when he asked the question, he would have stopped immediately but he went on with two or three more questions of the same type. As a result, in just a few seconds he had lost his case. He had irrevocably antagonised the jury.

If you are advancing a complex legal argument to a tribunal of law who may or may not have seen or read a skeleton argument in advance, you will understand (hopefully) the argument you are trying to present. The judge or judges may not, at least not at first.

Bear in mind that although judges are usually good lawyers and reasonably intelligent, their speed of thought is not instantaneous, particularly not with complex constructions. It may take them time to follow the argument. They may even wish to interrupt to ask you to clarify. If you are watching the judges, you will usually be able to see whether they are with you thus far before you move on to the next stage of the argument. This is particularly important if the judges, or some of them, do not agree with you. You may need to cover the point again from a different angle in order to try to get them to agree.

Rule 10: Keep it Short

When you wish to instruct, be brief; that men's ... minds take in quickly what you say, learn its lesson, and retain it faithfully. Every word that is unnecessary only pours over the side of a brimming mind.
Marcus Tullius Cicero

One of the standard techniques of rhetoric is to keep your sentences short and simple (see Rule 12 below). But the speech overall should be as short as is possible, consistent with covering all of the necessary points adequately. Repetition should be avoided.

One of the most important decisions in the whole of English legal history was the decision of Lord Mansfield CJ in the case of **Somerset v Stewart** (1772) 98 ER 499. This was the judgement which held that no one could lawfully be detained as a slave in England or forcibly removed from England on the basis that he was a slave. In effect, it held that slavery was unlawful in England.

It was a momentous decision. To have held that slavery was permissible would have been a moral disaster for the country but at that time a great deal of the British economy was dependent on the slave trade, so a decision that it was unlawful was likely to have major financial consequences.

It would have been difficult to find a better judge to take the decision than Lord Mansfield CJ. One of his favourite sayings, which he used in the case of **John**

Wilkes a few years earlier (1768) 98 ER 327 at 347) and again in a hearing in Somerset's case on 14 May 1772 was '*Fiat justitia ruat caelum*' (let justice be done, though the heavens fall).

Despite its huge importance and despite the fact that the language of 1772 had rather more embellishment than we use today, the judgement in Somerset's Case, which was delivered on 22 June 1772, is on a single page (p. 509 of the ER report). The essence of the decision is in the last few lines which contain only three sentences:

'*The state of slavery is of such a nature that it is incapable of being introduced on any reasons, moral or political, but only by positive law* [by which he meant an Act of Parliament] *which preserves its force long after the reasons, occasions and time itself from whence it was created, is erased from memory. It is so odious, that nothing can be suffered to support it, save positive law. Whatever inconveniences, therefore, may follow from the decision, I cannot say this case is allowed or approved by the Law of England and therefore the black must be discharged.*'

In those three sentences the judgement says all that is necessary. In fact, in modern language, we could say it in even shorter form:

'*The state of slavery is so odious that it could be made lawful only by an Act of Parliament and there is no such Act, so the state of slavery cannot exist in England and whatever the consequences, Mr Somerset must be released.*'

That is only one sentence. The point is the same on either version. If you can say it in one (or three) sentences, do not use two (or six).

Rule 11: Disguise Any Nerves

There are only two types of speakers in the world:
1. The nervous and 2. Liars.
Mark Twain

Everyone speaking in public is, or at least should be, nervous. A former Lord Chancellor, Lord Gerald Gardiner, once said at a Bar Mess: *'The day you stop being nervous as you rise to your feet in court, you will stop making a living at the Bar.'*

Nervousness in a capable speaker is not to be feared. It gives the speaker an adrenalin rush which speeds up the thought processes and sharpens the reactions. A first class speaker needs adrenalin.

Nevertheless, most people who are nervous make some movement because they are nervous. Almost everyone does it. Return to John F Kennedy's 'Berlin' speech. Look at his hands at the beginning of the speech. He was constantly adjusting his notes despite the fact that he was not looking at them. Although he was an outstandingly capable speaker, the movement he made was distracting (though, as he was addressing a very large mass audience, very few of them could see it).

Very many speakers put their hands to parts of the face or head, especially the hair, nose or ears. Some cough or make other small noises as though clearing the back of the throat. Others make adjustments to parts of their clothing. One of the worst habits is repeatedly clicking a retractable ballpoint pen. That introduces not only a distracting movement but also an irritating sound.

The eyes of hunting species such as humans are pre-programmed to be attracted by movement. That is why prey species, like rabbits, tend to freeze until the predator is almost upon them. The danger to a speaker is that if a nervous gesture is used which includes or consists of visible movement, especially movement of the hands near the face or head, it will distract the audience and is likely seriously to detract from the performance of the speaker. Even if the gesture is less obtrusive, if it is detected by the audience it gives away the fact that the speaker is nervous and detracts from the impression of confidence which most speakers are trying to achieve.

It is very difficult indeed to stop yourself using any nervous gesture but it is less difficult to train yourself to use a different gesture which is much less visible. Almost all the great advocates make nervous gestures but they are very difficult to detect because the great advocates deliberately train themselves to use nervous gestures which are not readily visible. One leading QC wrings his hands together but he does so between his back and his gown so the gesture is invisible from either front or back. Another transfers his weight from one foot to the other but without generating any visible movement. One of the greatest advocates of the present generation was once described as being rather like a swan in motion on the water: *'All smooth and unruffled where he is visible but paddling furiously underneath.'*

Rule 12: Learn and Use the Skills of Rhetoric

Rhetoric is the art of ruling the minds of men.
Plato

There are many rhetorical skills and devices. Some specialist texts on rhetoric list dozens. In an introductory work of this kind it is possible to deal with only a few – those judged to be the most important. We have already encountered three of them: the **repeated key phrase,** the **rhetorical question** and **inclusive language**. John F Kennedy used two of these techniques both at his inauguration speech and in the Berlin speech.

There are many technical (mostly Greek) terms for a **repeated key phrase.** If the repeat word or phrase is used at the beginning of each sentence or clause the term is **anaphora** or **epanophora**. If it comes at the end of each sentence or clause, the term is **antistrophe, epiphora** or **epistrophe** and, if it comes both at the beginning and at the end of each clause or sentence, the term is **symploce**.

'**Repeated key phrase**' is the authors' own term for this device. We use it: (a) because there are so many Greek terms for this device that it is difficult to know which to use, (b) as it is descriptive of its own definition, it is easier to remember and (c) it is applicable irrespective of the position of the repeat word or phrase.

An outstanding example is Churchill's *'We Shall Fight'* speech. In the nine sentences quoted earlier, the phrase appears seven times. The effect was so powerful that a substantial proportion of English speakers throughout the world know of the speech and refer to it by using that phrase.

One of the leading candidates for the greatest speech ever made is the Sermon on the Mount (Matthew, chapters 5 to 7). It has probably been repeated more than any other speech in history. It begins with the Beatitudes which are a near perfect example of the device:

Blessed are the poor in spirit:
*   for theirs is the Kingdom of heaven.*
Blessed are they that mourn:
*   for they shall be comforted.*
Blessed are the meek:
*   for they shall inherit the earth.*
Blessed are they which do hunger and thirst after righteousness:
*   for they shall be filled.*
Blessed are the merciful:
*   for they shall obtain mercy.*
Blessed are the pure in heart:
*   for they shall see God.*
Blessed are the peacemakers:
*   for they shall be called the children of God.*
Blessed are they which are persecuted for righteousness' sake:
*   for theirs is the Kingdom of heaven.*

Blessed are ye, when men shall revile you, and persecute you, and
*   shall say all manner of evil against you falsely, for my sake.*
Rejoice and be exceeding glad for great is your reward in heaven:
*   for so persecuted they the prophets which were before you.*

There is available online a short video extract from the film *Jesus of Nazareth* starring Robert Powell, in which the Beatitudes are delivered with superb voice control.

Another technique is called the '**rule of three**'. For whatever reason, the human brain responds very well to items in sets of three. For instance, if you wish to remember a long number sequence, it is easiest to do it in sets of three numbers. This fact can be used by a skilful speaker. One good example is Tony Blair's speech to the Labour Party Conference at Blackpool in October 1996:

'Ask me my three main priorities for government, and I tell you: education, education and education.'

It was no accident that he chose to refer to three main priorities and hence to use the word 'education' three times. He is an extremely capable public speaker and he was using a well-known rhetorical device.

Another example is the quotation from 1 Corinthians 13:13, so often used at weddings:

'In a word there are three things that last forever: faith, hope and love; but the greatest of these is love.' (***The New English Bible***: ***The Authorised Version*** refers to *'Faith, hope and charity'*.)

Another example, which lawyers encounter very frequently indeed is the witness oath:

'... the evidence I shall give shall be the truth, the whole truth and nothing but the truth'.

So, if you want to give heavy emphasis to a phrase, give it three elements. If you intend to repeat it for emphasis say it three times.

The rule also applies to the structure of a speech or an argument. The basic three part structure for a speech is discussed in Chapter 2. If you can put an argument under three main headings, do it and say you have done it. Then list your three headings before expanding on each of them. That will make the main structure of your address much easier to remember.

Next, the use of **contrasting phrases** (the technical term is **antithesis**).

A leading example is the Berlin Speech by President John F Kennedy referred to in relation to Rule 7 in which he repeatedly contrasted positive views of the communist regime with the phrase *'Let them come to Berlin'*. It is a particularly good example because he contrasted not only the words and meaning of the phrases but the meter in which they were expressed. The expressions describing the views of those with approval for the Communist system were in general fairly long sentences. *'Let them come to Berlin'* is very short and staccato and creates an abrupt contrast which was intended to reflect the contrast between the beliefs of anyone who expressed any faith in the Communist system and its harsh realities.

Almost 400 years earlier in 1588, the contrasting phrases technique was used by Elizabeth I at Tilbury in addressing her soldiers during the battle with the Armada:

'I know I have but the body of a weak and feeble woman; but I have the heart of a king, and of a King of England too ...'

The speech is set out with comments in the Appendix.

Another technique of rhetoric is sometimes referred to by the acronym **KISS** – keep it short and simple. That should apply to the whole speech (see Rule 10) and also to the phrases, sentences, and paragraphs within it.

Long rambling sentences should be avoided. One good example of a very long sentence is in the judgement of Lord Greene MR in the Court of Appeal decision in **C v C** (1921) 90 LJP 345 at p. 346. It is quoted in Sir Robert Megarry's book ***Miscellany at Law*** on p. 120. The case was a divorce based on an allegation of adultery and the issue was whether the wife and the co-respondent had managed to have sex on the front seat of a lorry under observation. Lord Greene observed:

'In view of the long history of passionate intimacy between the parties, to hold that these two persons could not have overcome such inconveniences as existed is in my opinion an inference which ought not to be drawn.'

That sentence contains 38 words. They are certainly memorable, they have elegance, charm and an element of humour but their meaning could expressed in far fewer words *'Yes, I think they probably did'*.

In general do not use more words than necessary, at least not until you have the verbal skills of Lord Greene.

The rule should not be applied universally. It can conflict with the requirement to use appropriate language. There are occasions when a more complex sentence construction will give a speech an air of gravity. The Churchill speech which was used in discussing Rule 4 contains a good example. Here is the text again:

'The gratitude of every home in our island, in our empire and indeed throughout the world, except in the abodes of the guilty, goes out to the British airmen who, undaunted by odds, unwearied in their constant challenge and mortal danger, are turning the tide of the World War by their prowess and by their devotion. Never in the field of human conflict was so much owed by so many to so few.'

Twelve Rules for Speaking in Public

This paragraph is 73 words long, yet it contains only two sentences. The first is 56 words long. It contains one main clause, two subordinate clauses and three other phrases, yet it does not sound at all overly long or pompous. Moreover, by using pauses skilfully, Churchill made the sentence sound much less complex than it is.

The benchmark is suitability. In general, do not use 38 words when six will do, but be prepared to use much more complex sentences when appropriate.

Next, **illustration**. Use **quotations**, **metaphors**, **similes** and **examples**. This technique is as old as oratory itself. Aristotle is quoted as having said *'The greatest thing by far is to have mastered the metaphor.'*

One outstanding example was the use by Winston Churchill in 1946 of the sentence:

'From Stettin in the Baltic to Trieste in the Adriatic, an iron curtain has descended across the continent.'

The power of the metaphor was such that the phrase *'The Iron Curtain'* has passed permanently into the language and is known throughout the world.

John F Kennedy made frequent use of metaphor including an advanced form of the technique in which two metaphors are used in quick succession which are also contrasting phrases. There is a good example in his inauguration speech:

'But this peaceful revolution of hope cannot become the prey of hostile powers.'

The authors' term for this device is the '**contrasting double metaphor**.'

Very few people have but the slightest fraction of Churchill's or of John Kennedy's skills as an orator and this book cannot hope to replicate them, but it does use some metaphorical expressions and a great many illustrations, largely by providing examples of the techniques it is suggested you use or of errors you are urged to avoid. It also uses a good many quotations. It is hoped that you agree that their use makes the text much easier to understand and to remember. The same applies to the content of a speech.

Poetry can be particularly effective in speeches, for example Robert Kennedy's quotation from Aeschylus in the speech referred to in the section on Rule 5.

Use **humour**. Again, its use needs to be suitable. Humour is sometimes a requirement. Gerard Hoffnung's speech to the Oxford Union is a prime example, as is any speech made in an after-dinner context. Humour in a political speech can be very effective indeed. Humour in a court context has to be rather more restrained but even here it has its uses. George Carman QC, in the closing speech to the jury in his successful defence of the comedian, Ken Dodd, on tax evasion charges in 1989, caused some amusement when he used the sentence: *'Some accountants are* *comedians but comedians are never accountants.'* How much effect it had on the decision will never be known but he did win the case.

Next, **voice modulation**. Obviously you should not deliver any speech in a monotone. It is necessary to vary the tone, pitch, volume and speed of your voice as you proceed.

First, identify the words you intend to use and the effect you intend to achieve. If you wish to raise emotions, raise your voice, speak a little faster (though never too fast) and emphasise the consonants. If you wish to soothe, then reduce both the volume and the pace and extend the vowels.

An outstanding example is the recitation by the actor, Richard Burton, of the poem by Dylan Thomas 'Do Not Go Gentle Into That Good Night'. A sound recording is available online. Listen to it. It is worth doing so more than once. It is only a short recording but the way in which the volume, intonation and pace of the voice are altered and the way the actor pauses are a very fine illustration of how it should be done.

Irony can also be an extremely useful oratorical tool. Try by way of example Mark Anthony's speech from Shakespeare's play *Julius Caesar* which begins: *'Friends, Romans, countrymen'* (several recordings are available online).

In the speech, the phrase: '*Brutus is an honourable man*' is repeated four times in conjunction with either '*the noble Brutus hath told you Caesar was ambitious*' or '*but Brutus says he was ambitious*'. This is yet another example of the repeated key phrase but these repetitions are interspersed with reminders of things Caesar had done which suggested strongly that he was anything but ambitious and that Brutus was anything but honourable. The irony becomes steadily more and more apparent with the repetitions.

Another effective technique is to use and to repeat a key phrase but to invert it on repetition. The technical term is **antimetabole** or **chiasmus**.

There is a very good example in John F Kennedy's inauguration speech:

'*And so my fellow Americans, ask not what your country can do for you but what you can do for your country.*'

It is followed by a pair of contrasting phrases in which the inverted phrase is repeated in its original form:

'*My fellow citizens of the world, ask not what America will do for you, but what together we can do for the freedom of man.*'

As well as the antimetabole for which the speech is chiefly remembered, numerous other oratorical devices were used. There were many uses of **inclusive language** as was advised in Rule 3: '*our ancient heritage*', *'we are committed'*. There were numerous metaphors: *'that torch has been passed on to a new generation of Americans'*, *'the glow from that fire can truly light the world'* and the contrasting double metaphor quoted a little earlier in this section. The speech was also delivered with very careful pausing, highly effective voice modulation and emphatic use of the hands.

Next, what are sometimes referred to as **sonic devices**, for example **alliteration**, **assonance** and **onomatopoeia**, may on occasions be used in a speech. They are more often found in poetry but they can also be useful in addressing an audience in public. If, for example, you are referring to a crime involving the deliberate sale to members of the public of many defective cars, a phrase like *'dishonest duplicated double dealing'* will be more memorable than *'repetitive fraud'*.

Finally, there is the **rhetorical question** (putting what is in reality a statement into the form of a question to which the speaker does not expect a reply, with the implication that no reply is needed because the answer is obvious. The technical term is **erotema**). *'Given the evidence in this case, members of the jury, I submit that my client cannot be convicted'* would be far less effective in a closing speech for the defence than *'given the evidence in this case, members of the jury, how can you possibly convict the defendant?'*.

As another example, suppose that you were asked to make a speech at a function seeking donations to a fund for the support of the families of members of the armed forces who have lost their lives in the service of the country. You could end by quoting the verse from the poem 'For the Fallen' composed by Lawrence Binion in 1914, which is recited on Remembrance Day every year, but invert the last line to produce a rhetorical question:

They shall grow not old as we who are left grow old:
Age shall not weary them, nor the years condemn.
At the going down of the sun and in the morning
Will we remember them?

CHAPTER 2

PREPARING A SPEECH

It usually takes more than three weeks
to prepare a good impromptu speech.
Mark Twain

1. Identify the Purpose of the Speech

The better shall my purpose work on him.
William Shakespeare, *Othello*

The first step in constructing a speech, and a vital one, is to identify precisely what you want the presentation of the speech to achieve. What is the purpose of the speech? For example, if you are delivering the best man's speech at a wedding, you have three objectives:

1) To pay a tribute to the happy couple,
2) To amuse those present at the reception,
3) To propose a toast.

These objectives will define both the content and the structure of the speech.

If the occasion is a political speech, there may well be only one object, to persuade the electorate to vote for you.

If it is a closing speech for the defence in a criminal trial the sole object will be to maximise the defendant's chances of acquittal.

2. The Three Part Structure

If you have an important point to make, don't try to be
subtle or clever. Use a pile driver. Hit the point once.
Then come back and hit it again. Then hit it a
third time – a tremendous whack.
Winston Churchill

In **Rhetorica,** Cicero listed what he called: *'the six parts of a discourse'*:

1)   Introduction
2)   Statement of Facts
3)   Division
4)   Proof
5)   Refutation
6)   Conclusion.

He said the introduction was intended to obtain the attention of the audience, the statement of facts was a recitation of the relevant history, division was the identification of what was in issue and what was not, proof consisted of the arguments and evidence, refutation was the destruction of the opposing arguments and conclusion was the end of the speech composed as directed by the principles of rhetoric.

In more recent times it has often been said that, just as a good concerto should contain three movements, a good speech should contain three sections:

Preparing a Speech

1) Introduction
2) Body
3) Conclusion.

In this format, the body of the speech would include Cicero's Statement of Facts, Division, Proof and Refutation, to the extent that each of them is required in the relevant context.

The three part structure is not of universal application. Nevertheless, it represents an appropriate starting point for almost any speech and it can be modified as the occasion demands.

3. The Introduction

There are two things which I am confident I can do very well; one is an introduction to any literary work, stating what it is to contain, and how it should be executed in the most perfect manner.
Samuel Johnson

The main purpose of the introduction is to give the audience a summary of what you intend to say in the main body of the speech. In addition, so far as relevant, you should:

1) Start by capturing the attention of the audience.
2) Tell the audience who you are.
3) Tell them why you are qualified to speak on the subject you are to address.
4) Tell them how they will benefit from hearing what you have to say – give them a reason to listen.

Having done that, you should list the topics you intend to cover, or the arguments you intend to present in the main body of the speech.

If possible, you should begin with a sentence or paragraph which has sufficient impact to capture the attention of the audience and hopefully make it clear that they have no need to fear that they may be bored by the remainder of what you have to say.

For example, in a speech on road safety you might begin by saying *'This speech will last ten minutes. In that time, around the world xxx people will die in road accidents.'*

Preparing a Speech

This has immediate impact, though you should check the up-to-date statistics and get the figures correct and make a note of where you obtained them so that if anyone challenges the figures you can support what you have said.

Other useful attention-grabbing devices are a question, either real or rhetorical, or an appropriate quotation or a poem. For example, you could begin a speech on the importance of lifelong learning with: *'Eartha Kitt once said: "I am learning all the time. The tombstone will be my diploma."'*

Given a good quality dictionary of quotations, it is relatively easy to find a quotation on almost any topic. Try to choose one that relates directly to your subject and if possible choose one from somebody whose name will be recognised by your audience.

To begin with a poem is more difficult for two reasons: first, an appropriate poem can be hard to find and to write one is very difficult indeed. Second, if you use a poem, it must be short. However, it can be done and when an appropriate poem can be found it can be very effective.

For instance, the speech for the fund to support the families of the fallen referred to at the end of the previous chapter could begin with the well-known lines by Rupert Brooke:

Advocacy and Public Speaking

'If I should die think only this of me: That there's some corner of a foreign field that is forever England.'

It is almost always unwise to begin by using phrases such as *'I am going to begin with a question'* or *'I am going to begin with a quotation'*. To do so reduces the impact almost totally. Just ask the question or launch into the quotation. If you wish to explain its relevance to what you have to say, do so after the question or quotation, not before.

In many cases you will need to introduce yourself to the audience and explain why you are qualified to speak on your subject. For example, if you are giving a lecture on the need for students to stay clear of recreational drugs, you might say:

'My name is XXXX; I am a consultant psychiatrist. In the last 20 years I have dealt with over 5,000 patients whose lives have been destroyed by drug addiction. Eight-five per cent of them began their descent into serious drug abuse by taking recreational drugs at parties.'

This is not a universal rule and can be modified to suit the circumstances. When Neil Armstrong made a speech about space exploration, he did not need to tell the audience who he was or why he felt qualified to speak on the subject.

Yet again, suitability is the key. Choose the elements the occasion requires. As an example, if your speech is to be made in Manchester on 'how to protect your home from burglars', you might say:

'I expect this speech to last about 15 minutes. On average in Greater Manchester, five homes will be burgled while I speak. My object in making this speech is to enable you to reduce the possibility that your home will be one of them. My name is Mark Morris. I was for 25 years a member of the Greater Manchester Police Force. I retired 10 years ago as a Detective Chief Inspector. Since then I have been a consultant to three companies who specialise in the provision and installation of domestic security systems. In this presentation I intend to explain the details of five devices you can use to protect your home and why each is effective. The five devices are: (List).'

4. The Body of the Speech

Let thy speech be short, comprehending much in few words.
Ecclesiasticus 32:8

In order to compose the body of the speech, you will need to research, select and assemble the material or the arguments you wish to advance, together with the evidence in support of each point. You then need to decide on a logical order. If it is a humorous speech, you need to assemble, order and present the jokes and anecdotes you wish to include. As before, everything is dictated by the purpose of the speech.

In assembling the material, Chapter 1: Rule 1 (prepare thoroughly) is highly relevant. The more studious you have been in your preparation, the better your research in advance has been, the more material and evidence, humorous anecdotes, or legal authorities you have been able to assemble, the better the speech is likely to be.

In addition, if you have researched thoroughly and assembled a large volume of relevant material, you can then obey the 'Keep it Short' rule by selecting the funniest, the most relevant, the most persuasive or the most memorable material. That will inevitably raise the quality of the speech.

A good rule of thumb is to assemble enough material for a speech about two and a half times as long as you intend it to be and then prune it ruthlessly to the length required. Do be ruthless. In public speaking, Oliver

Preparing a Speech

Wendell Holmes's quotation: *'A day's impact is better than a month of dead pull'* could be re-written as *'a minute's impact is much better than an hour of monotony'*. A speech lasting 10 minutes and making three points, all of which the audience remember, is better than one lasting an hour and making 18 points, of which they remember only one. Andrew Carnegie, the Scottish/American steel millionaire once said:

'A speaker who does not strike oil in ten minutes should stop boring.'

Having assembled and selected the material you intend to use, you must then put it into some sort of logical order. There is no universal rule about how the order should be determined. It might be chronological, topical, spatial or indeed any other order which suits the material and the occasion. If you have a story to tell, chronological order would probably be the best. If you are presenting the results of scientific research at a conference then it would probably be best to adopt a problem-research-results-conclusions structure. The Best Man's speech referred to in the first paragraph of this chapter would probably be best arranged thematically. Once again 'suitability' (Cicero would have said 'decorum') is the key.

When you present the material by delivering the speech, follow the Twelve Rules discussed in Chapter 1 and use the rhetorical skills and devices listed in Rule 12, especially examples. In many contexts it will also be sensible to use visual aids.

Advocacy and Public Speaking

A great many speakers rely on statistics to back up what they say. To do so can be very effective indeed but make sure they are from a reputable source, make sure they are relevant and make sure you have a detailed note of where you found them.

You should also consider the use of anything else which will illustrate the message you intend to convey, such as PowerPoint or other visual aids, sound or video recordings or even practical demonstrations. The Royal Institution Christmas Lectures for Children are prime examples of the efficacy of demonstration.

5. Refutation

*... we stood talking for some time of Bishop Berkeley's
ingenious sophistry to prove the non-existence of matter,
and that every thing in the universe is merely ideal. I
observed that although we are satisfied his doctrine is
not true, it is impossible to refute it. I shall never forget
the alacrity with which Johnson answered, striking
his foot with mighty force against a large stone, till
he rebounded from it, 'I refute it* thus'.*
James Boswell, *Life of Johnson*

In some types of speech, you will be required not
merely to present your own arguments but also to
refute those advanced by your opponents. This is true
of legal cases, moots, debates and many political
speeches.

If you are required to refute you should:

(a) Refer to any positive material or evidence which
     tends to disprove your opponent's case. For
     example:

*'The prosecution allege that this crime was committed in the
library with the lead piping. Yet stains of blood which DNA
analysis has established is that of the victim were found on
the carpet in the study.'*

(b) Point out and emphasise any errors in your
     opponent's arguments. Here is another example:

'The prosecution say that while none of the items of evidence available in this case would, by itself, prove the guilt of the defendant, the accumulation of all of it is sufficient to do so. That argument might work if there were any value at all in any of the individual points. If you accumulate a large quantity of pennies, you may achieve a total of several pounds. However, every item of this prosecution case is rubbish and if you accumulate a large number of small piles of rubbish, all you get is a bigger pile of rubbish.'

6. The Conclusion

You should end by summarising what you have presented in the body of the speech. By doing so, you will reinforce your message and make the points more memorable. In short, the three part structure involves:

a) Telling the audience what you are going to say.
b) Saying it.
c) Summarising what you have said.

If possible, you should end as you began: by using an expression which captures the attention of the audience and which they will remember later. You should make it obvious, without saying it, that your speech is over. As with the opening, you could use a quotation, a few lines from a poem, a rhetorical question or something of that nature. The very well-known *'I have a dream'* speech made by Dr Martin Luther King at a civil rights march in Washington on 28 March 1963 ends with a quotation from a Negro Spiritual. 'Free *at last'*. A speech on the importance of lifelong learning might end:

'Albert Einstein once said, "Intellectual growth should commence at birth and cease only at death." As far as I can see from here, not one of you is dead yet.'

If you intend to thank the audience or to invite questions, do so after you have delivered the concluding expression and after the applause which (hopefully) it generates, not before.

CHAPTER 3

PREPARING A CASE FOR COURT

The armourers, accomplishing the Knights,
With busy hammers closing rivets up,
Give dreadful note of preparation.
William Shakespeare, *Henry V*

1. The Scope of this Chapter

This chapter is intended to explain the general strategic approach required in preparing a legal case of almost any kind. While references are made to the relevant rules of court and to decisions of a procedural kind already made by the court, it is beyond the scope of this book, and hence of this chapter, to deal in detail with the specific procedural requirements of any particular type of case. For that, you should refer to one of the practitioners' books on the subject, any of which will be considerably larger than this volume.

2. Begin with the Basics

Before any decisions can be taken about:

i)   Whether a case is viable,
ii) How to prepare and present it if it is viable, or
iii) What to do if it appears not to be viable,

– the basic structure of the case must be ascertained.

In most cases the basic steps will have been taken before the papers are put before an advocate. However, the required steps are as follows:

a)   Identify the type of case – criminal, family, civil, tribunal, etc.
b)   Ascertain the role of the lay client[1] in the proceedings – prosecutor or defendant, applicant or respondent, claimant or defendant, etc.
c)   Find out what case the lay client wishes to make or what case he or she has to answer and what that answer is. For example, she is a graphic designer who has not been paid for her work and wishes to make a claim for the money, or he is a defendant in criminal proceedings in which he is charged with burglary and denies ever entering the building which was burgled.

---

[1] This expression is used by a barrister to refer to the person for whom he or she is acting. The solicitor who instructs the barrister on behalf of the lay client is referred to as the professional client.

d) Make an assessment of the actual or likely strength of the opposing case. If you are defending the burglar, obtain the prosecution advance disclosure. This will enable you to see the main strength of the case against him more or less at the outset. If you are acting for the unpaid graphic designer in a civil case you will probably be dependent at first on her account and the strength of the opposing case may only emerge at a later stage.

e) Take a statement from the lay client giving the basic factual substrate of the case and the lay client's factual assertions either explaining the case to be advanced or the answer to the case to be met.

f) Identify any other potential useful witnesses and if possible obtain statements from them.

g) Identify and preserve any relevant documentation.

h) If the case is subject to any pre-action protocol, make sure it is complied with.

i) If the case is of a type in which formal notices of application, claim forms or statements of case are required, draft, file and serve these in accordance with the rules of the court.

j) If the court rules, or any order a court has already made, require disclosure of any witness statements or documents, make sure this is done as required.

k) Consider whether any expert evidence is likely to be required.

3. Prepare Thoroughly

... for a wide knowledge is needed to give a luxuriance and richness to language which, unless the speaker has thoroughly mastered his subject, suffers from what I may perhaps call a puerile vapidity of expression.
Marcus Tullius Cicero

In this field, as in relation to every other topic in this book, thorough preparation is vital. At whatever stage you enter the case, start by reading everything you have and double-check that none of the material which ought to be in the file as a result of the steps listed in section 2 is missing or deficient. If there is anything missing, make good the deficit (or have it made good) as quickly as possible.

As part of your preparation, it is essential that you check on the relevant area or areas of law involved in the case and make sure you have a thorough working knowledge of all the relevant areas. The next step in the process is to devise a strategy, and you need to be able to devise a strategy which is both factually and legally sound.

4. Devise a Strategy – Start at the End

Start at the end! At first, this may sound very strange but in order to prepare and present a legal case, it is essential to think strategically. To devise a strategy you need first to identify the objective and then to plan how to achieve it. Although it sounds peculiar to start at the end and work towards the beginning, this is a widely used technique usually called 'Backward Planning'.

To identify the objective you need to establish:

(a) Who is going to take the relevant decision?
(b) What is the nature of the decision they are to take?
(c) What do you want them to decide? (If you are to win.)

Although this analysis involves three stages, it can be summarised in the single question:

Q1: 'Who do I have to convince, and of what, in order to win this case?'

There are almost as many possible answers to this question as there are cases in court but the question is nearly always the same. Having answered it you will have identified the objective of your efforts.

The only significant variation is that the word 'win' is not apposite where there is no real contest in the case, for example in the Crown Court in prosecuting or defending in a case where the defendant has pleaded guilty and the court is merely deciding the appropriate sentence. In such a case, for 'win' substitute 'achieve the desired result in'. As you can see the substitution makes no real difference to the nature of the question.

Next, you need to consider how to achieve the result and you continue Backward Planning. Start by considering your closing address to the tribunal you have to convince and ask yourself the second question:

Q2: 'How can I address the tribunal in a way which is likely to convince them and what material do I need in order to be able to make that address?'

The task is to devise a final speech with a reasonable prospect of success which you are likely to be able to make on the basis of the available material, taking account of what you already have and what you think you are likely to be able to obtain.

Having devised the intended closing speech, the next stage is to consider what material you need to support it.

The question of what material you 'need' should be addressed on two levels:

1) What is the minimum requirement to enable the argument to be presented in a manner which has a reasonable prospect of success?

2) What additional material might feasibly be available which it would be advisable to have if it can be obtained?

The answer to that question should lead you to a list of the material you 'need' on each level.

5. If There is no Workable Strategy

When you have considered questions one and two above, you may come to the conclusion that there is no available strategy which has any real chance of success. Return to the defence of the alleged burglar. Suppose that you discover that there is clear evidence that his fingerprints have been found on the inside of the safe at the premises and some of the stolen property has been found at his home. He has no explanation for the presence of his fingerprints or for the presence of the property at his house.

In such a case, arrange to see the client as soon as possible, advise him that in your judgement his case is likely to fail and try to persuade him to cooperate in a damage limitation exercise. If the case is a civil one, obtain instructions to settle it on the best terms available. If it is a criminal defence case, advise the client of the reduction in sentence likely to be achieved by somebody who pleads guilty early on.

If the client agrees to deal with the matter by way of damage limitation, the objective to be achieved will have changed. It may be that the new strategy involves action other than presenting the case in court, such as negotiating a settlement. If some sort of court hearing is still required, then the same questions need to be re-asked in relation to the new objective. In the burglary case, the initial answer to Q1 was *'I need to persuade the jury that there is or may be some explanation for the presence of the fingerprints in the safe and the property in my client's house other than that he is guilty of the burglary'.* Instead, it has now become: *'I need to persuade the judge that the least possible sentence will meet the justice of the case.'*

If the client will not agree to amend the objective then you will just have to devise the best strategy you can with what you have. You will know from the outset that your efforts are likely to fail. You must get used to that. As a professional advocate you cannot hope to win every case you undertake, particularly not for clients who will not take your advice. It is no adverse reflection on a professional advocate that he or she loses a case which deserved to lose, especially not if he or she has identified early on that failure was likely and has advised the client accordingly. Bill Jones, who was for many years the clerk to the barristers' chambers at 39 Whitefriars, and later at Sedan House, Chester, who had spent the Second World War in a cavalry regiment and who took part in the last cavalry charge ever made by the British Army, was often heard to use the metaphor *'You can't come without the horse'.*

6. Advise the Lay Client of the Risks.

Even if there is a workable strategy, it is highly unlikely that you will be certain of success. In addition, unless you already have all the material you 'need' in both lists, the chances of success will be dependent on whether the extra material still required can be obtained. Your knowledge of the strength of the opposing case may also be incomplete, particularly in the early stages.

The lay client needs to be advised as to your assessment of the chances of success, conditional if necessary on getting any additional information or evidence. You will probably also need to include an analysis of the state of the relevant law (see Chapter 4) and you will need to include any uncertainty as to the state of the law in your assessment of the chances of success.

You will also need to keep the lay client informed throughout of what he or she is likely to gain if they win or the loss (including the costs) if they fail and you need to obtain specific instructions to proceed on that basis. This will be done either by seeing the client in conference, or by written advice or letter.

7. Continue Reverse Planning

The answers to questions 1 and 2 should have led you to a list of the material you need on each of the two levels that 'need' has been defined. The next question is rather more complex:

Q3: (a) To what extent do I have this material already?

   (b) To the extent that I do have this material, where is it?

   (c) To the extent that I do not have this material, can I get it and, if so, where and how?

   (d) How am I going to make sure that this material is properly before the court by the end of the hearing?

Usually, some of the material you need will already be in your possession. It is likely to consist either of the documents or the potential oral evidence of witnesses as set out in their witness statements. All you need to do to get this before the court or tribunal is to prove and produce the documents and to call the witnesses.

For example, consider the unpaid graphic designer and let us assume that the defendant agrees that there was a contract and that he has not paid, but denies the detail you allege as to the terms of the contract and says that in any event the work was so badly done as to be useless. This is a common defence raised in cases of this kind.

On those facts the answer to Q1 was: *'I need to persuade the judge that the claimant has a right to be paid.'*

The answer to Q2 was: *'I need to be able to address the judge at the end of the case and to say that it has been proved that:*

1) *The terms of the contract as to the work to be done and as to payment were as my lay client alleges,*
2) *The claimant fulfilled the contract terms, and*
3) *Her work was satisfactory.*

To do that I need:

a) *If the contract was written, the contractual documents including the details of the work to be done and the terms as to payment. If it was oral, the evidence of the lay client and anybody else who was present as to what was said.*
b) *Evidence that the work was completed.*
c) *Evidence that the standard of the work was at least adequate and preferably better than that.'*

Let us assume that the contract was contained in three letters and that the lay client has already given you copies of:

i)   The initial letter from the customer asking her to quote for the work,
ii) The quotation she sent in response which includes details of the work to be done and the terms as to payment, and
iii) The letter from the customer accepting the terms of the quotation.

71

That should prove item 1).

As to 2), her own witness statement will contain the evidence that she did the work and much of the work she did will be printable material which will be readily available. This can all be dealt with simply by calling your lay client as a witness and having her produce the documents.

Some of the material you 'need' may be in the items filed or served by the other side. In the graphic designer case, a witness statement by the customer's secretary may contain some evidence of the claimant's completion of the work. Or the contract may include some documents which are produced by the opposition.

If this is the case, you need to take steps to make sure that the material is before the court when you make your closing speech. If the material is documentary and if it contains only information helpful to you, you should agree the documents. If the material is in a witness statement which contains nothing you need to contradict, agree the witness statement.

If the documents contain a mixture of helpful and adverse material you will need to agree that the documents should be admitted but not agree that their contents are accurate. If the witness statement contains a mixture of helpful and hostile material, you will need to insist that the witness is called.

Turning to the material you do not yet have, return to the two lists of items you 'need' and identify which of them you have yet to obtain and how to obtain them. In the case of the graphic designer, you have some evidence that the work was adequately completed but clearly more is needed. It would for instance be wise to check whether the client kept a diary or any other record of the hours she spent working on this project. It is likely that she did, so ask her and get the records produced, filed at court and served on the defendant. A supplemental witness statement may well be required to produce the relevant material. Additionally, can any of her staff support her as to what was done and how long it took? Did any of the staff do some of the work? Did she show the work to anybody else? If the answer to any of these questions is in the affirmative, witness statements will be required.

It would obviously also be wise to obtain an expert report on the standard of the work done. You will need to identify a suitable expert, decide whether the rules of court require the expert to be appointed on a joint basis or whether each side is likely to have their own expert. In either case, do you need permission from the court? If so, you will need to apply for permission. If one expert for each side is permitted, it is customary for the two experts to meet to discuss the issues between them and for them to produce a joint report setting out the points of agreement and disagreement with brief reasons for the latter. This needs to be arranged and if necessary ordered by the court.

If an expert is required, make very sure the person you choose to instruct is adequately qualified. A witness may be qualified by virtue of education, training, research or experience or by virtue of anything else which equips him or her adequately to address the problem. However, the possession of adequate expertise is essential. There are significant numbers of people who put themselves forward to act as expert witnesses on many subjects, usually for very substantial fees, who do not possess adequate skills. Such a witness is unlikely to survive cross-examination by an opposing advocate who has been briefed by an expert who does have adequate skills. This is a particular hazard in the field of accident investigation. It is not uncommon to find witnesses with significant experience but little formal training who apply equations relating to motion by rote without any real understanding of what each equation means or when not to use it.

8. If a Legal Argument is Needed

If a legal argument is required, prepare it. This is a highly specialised skill and Chapter 4 is specifically devoted to it.

The fact that it is dealt with only very briefly in this chapter does not mean that it should be overlooked. In addition to assembling the legal argument and the authorities in support of it, you are likely to be required by the rules of court to file a skeleton argument in advance and this will need to be drafted. Chapter 5 deals with how to do this.

9. Keep Reassessing the Chances of Success

If the advice given earlier was conditional on further evidence being available, the chances of success should be reviewed as you discover whether it is or is not available and advise the lay client accordingly. You may well be able to tell him or her at the outset:

'If we can get A, B and C we can probably win this case.'

You may then discover on investigation that some or all of the material cannot be obtained or that the opposing case is much stronger than you expected. Another possibility is that additional material you tried to obtain harms rather than helps your case. For example, in the graphic designer case, a jointly instructed expert is appointed and reports that her work was indeed defective.

In those circumstances you must be prepared to tell the lay client:

'I said that if we could get A, B and C we would probably succeed but in the event they are not available and in light of that I assess the chances of success at only X%.'

or:

'I said that if we could get an expert report confirming that your work was of satisfactory quality we could probably succeed but in the event that is not what the expert has said and in the light of that we are not likely to succeed.'

Whether you advise switching to a damage limitation strategy will depend on how much of the evidence has proved to be unobtainable or unhelpful, and the extent to which the chances of success have been reduced.

10. Refutation

Having dealt with everything else, the next main question is:

Q4: 'What parts of my opponent's evidence do I need to refute/challenge and how do I go about it?'

Again there are almost as many answers to this question as there are cases but the question is almost always the same. You need at least to challenge and if possible to rebut anything which is contrary to your lay client's case, either factually or legally. If it is a legal contradiction it will be dealt with in your legal argument as to which you should read the next chapter. If it is a factual contradiction, you need to deal with it using the evidence. There are five main methods of doing so:

a) Produce other evidence which directly contradicts the evidence you disagree with.

b) Produce other evidence which, while it does not directly contradict the evidence with which you disagree, tends to throw doubt on its veracity or reliability.

c) Try to cross-examine the witness who gives the evidence you need to refute into changing his or her mind.

d) Try, in cross-examination, to throw doubt on the reliability or veracity of the evidence on the basis of factors relating to the evidence itself.

e) Try, in cross-examination, to throw doubt on the reliability or veracity of the evidence on the basis of factors relating to the witness.

Of these, the first two are overwhelmingly the most effective. The vast majority of cases are won as a result of the positive evidence produced in support of the argument relied on rather than as a result of damage done to the opponent's case.

As to a), let us assume you are dealing with a claim for damages for personal injuries arising from a motor accident. Your client is the claimant and her case is that as she was driving along the main road a car driven by the defendant came from the opposite direction round the corner ahead of her on the wrong side of the road and hit her. The other driver's case is that he was not on the wrong side of the road, she was. The obvious possible sources of evidence are any eyewitnesses, especially independent witnesses who were not in either car, or some evidence that there are skid marks or debris on the road which tends to suggest where the point of impact was. Are there any photographs showing skid marks?

Another obvious example of direct contradiction is an alibi defence in a criminal case. In one case many years ago at Knutsford Crown Court, a defendant's defence to a charge of murder was that he could not have been guilty of a murder committed in Altrincham because at the relevant time he was committing a burglary in Birmingham. It was not only a very unusual alibi; it was also a particularly difficult one to present, because the other burglars, not unnaturally, were not willing to identify themselves by giving evidence in support of it. Nevertheless, defence counsel was able to produce police evidence from the burglary case that the defendant's fingerprints had been found at the burglary scene in circumstances where they must have been made by one of the burglars and he was also able to establish that the burglary and the murder occurred at about the same time. As a result the defence succeeded.

As to calling other evidence which tends to cast doubt on the veracity or reliability of the evidence you disagree with, a good example is a criminal case tried at Caernarfon Crown Court some years ago in which two men were charged with robbing an elderly man of an antique oak chest. His evidence was that he answered the door to them and that they barged past him and took the chest from his front room despite his protests. Their case was that they had offered to buy it, that he had agreed and that they had paid the agreed price.

The defence solicitor was particularly thorough and had placed advertisements for witnesses in the local press. As a result, defence counsel was able to call evidence from the alleged victim's brother-in-law that the morning after the chest had left the alleged victim's possession, he had told the brother-in-law that the men had called offering to buy old furniture and that he had got what he regarded as a very good price for the chest. When he had told the brother-in-law what the price was, the brother-in-law had said to him that the chest was worth very much more than the figure quoted and the complaint of robbery was made within an hour or so after that.

Note that this was not evidence directly contradicting the alleged victim's account because the brother-in-law was not present when the chest was taken from the house. It was evidence that the alleged victim had made a statement on another occasion which was seriously inconsistent with his evidence in support of the prosecution case. It also provided a clear reason why the story might have changed and why the evidence given in court might well be seriously unreliable.

That this conversation had occurred was put to the alleged victim in cross-examination, but he denied it. When the brother-in-law was called as a witness for the defence and gave his account it was scarcely surprising that the defendants were acquitted in short order.

Occasionally, it may be possible to rebut part of your opponent's case using one of his own witnesses. In one case tried at Mold Crown Court about 25 years ago an assault on the victim had been seen by four eyewitnesses. Two of them identified the defendant as the culprit on an identification parade. Only those two were called by the Crown. Counsel for the defence discovered that the other two had not merely failed to identify anybody; they had each made what purported to be a positive identification of a person who was not the defendant. Moreover, each of the two witnesses had positively identified the same member of the parade.

Counsel for the defence required the officer who had conducted the identification parade to be called as a prosecution witness and in cross-examination asked him about the identification by the other two witnesses, which he admitted had occurred.

Counsel for the defence therefore argued that there was just as good a case against person X as there was against the defendant. The defendant was acquitted.

Items c), d) and e) are matters for cross-examination, so they are dealt with in Chapter 6.

11. Presentation

When all these processes are complete, you need to assemble all the evidence and legal material and decide in what order you will call or produce the evidence. If an opening speech or statement is needed, write it. When that is complete you are, or should be, ready for trial.

CHAPTER 4

HOW TO RESEARCH, ASSEMBLE AND PRESENT

A LEGAL ARGUMENT

*If we knew what it was we were doing, it would not
be called research, would it?*

Albert Einstein

1. Introduction

Legal research is usually undertaken by a student preparing for:

(a)   a coursework essay
(b)   a coursework problem question
(c)   a moot or
(d)   a mock trial.

Legal research is usually undertaken by a practitioner:

(e)   in order to advise a client (personally or in writing) on the prospects of success for his or her case

or

(f)   in preparation for a legal argument in court.

In order to achieve any of these, the following steps are required:

Preparation:

(a)   Identify the area of law concerned.

84

(b) Acquire sufficient knowledge of the basic structure of the relevant area of law to enable you to carry out the research process in an intelligent way.

Research:

(c) Look for and identify the primary sources of law on the subject. These will be legislation or delegated legislation, decided cases or (in rare instances) long established custom.

(d) Extract from the primary sources the specific words relevant to your specific problem.

(e) Identify any relevant material which is not a primary source but may be persuasive.

Assembly:

(f) Arrange the material you have obtained in a logical order.

Analysis:

(g) Decide what conclusion as to the state of the law can be reached from the material in the primary sources. This will involve not only analysis of 'what the answer is' but also how firmly the answer can be stated. There will be many cases in which the conclusion is that the law is uncertain.

(h) Apply the answer to your specific problem.

Presentation:

(i) Write the essay, answer the problem question, advise the client or argue the case,

or

(j) Present the extracts from the primary sources and any other useful material to the court, moot or mock trial in a logical way in an effort to persuade the relevant tribunal that the law supports your client's case or that the argument you have been told to present is correct.

Amongst students there is a common conception that the legal research required for an essay is different from that required to deal with a problem question and that the research undertaken by a student differs from that undertaken by a practitioner. It is not clear where this idea originates but, whatever its origins, the conception is wrong. The preparation, assembly, analysis and presentation may vary but the process of research itself does not. Exactly the same steps are required in all cases.

Take, for example, a set of facts which raise questions about the jurisdiction of the courts in proceedings for Judicial Review on Proportionality grounds. In the case of either a problem question or an essay a student would be expected to demonstrate knowledge of the origins of the doctrine of proportionality and provide some context and background to the topic, followed by analysis of the main cases in that area. A practitioner would perhaps not need to demonstrate knowledge of the background or the history, but certainly would need to demonstrate to the client (and in due course to the court) a sufficient grasp of the present state of the law on the subject to be able to cope with the case. The order in which the available material is presented might differ as between an essay, the answer to a problem question or advice to a client, but this would not change the nature of the research required.

For a new student, legal research is a daunting task but before you climb up to the 10-metre board and dive into a confusing and very deep pool of text and materials, pause for a moment and consider what the task requires. Some students may consider the preliminary stages of research a waste of valuable time, especially when a deadline for submission is looming. However, as you will see in the remainder of this chapter, the preparation stage is vital and will aid you not only in your research but also in the organisation and presentation of your results. It is essential to remember that time spent in planning and preparing for your research will save you time in the longer run.

When you come to present the material, in whatever form, the presentation will require a structure. You could leave this until after you have assembled the relevant material but it is much better in almost all cases to devise the structure at the outset. You can then conduct your research in accordance with the structure.

This will act as a guide to what you need to research, and will hopefully ensure that nothing vital is missed. It will also mean that when you reach the end of the search process the material you have obtained will already be in a reasonably logical order and only minor adjustments will be needed.

The advice which follows is a generic guide on how to conduct research. It does not deal with any specific subject area though it does use some specific examples. The authors hope that this will guide the preparation of the majority of undergraduate assignments, as well as teaching the basic research skills required for success as a practitioner.

2. Preparation

Before you begin research it is essential that you have an adequate understanding of the relevant area of law sufficient to enable you to navigate through the process of research. Do not be tempted to omit this first step. If you do, you will be trying to navigate without a compass.

By the time you are a practitioner, even a fairly newly qualified one, once you have established the basic facts of a case, it is likely that you will already have sufficient knowledge of the basic structure of the main topics of the law to be able to identify, in general terms, what the relevant area of law is so step (a) will not be required. As to step (b), you probably will need to obtain a practitioners' textbook on the subject and read up on the details so that you can cope with the legal complexities of the case.

As a student, start with common sense. Almost certainly the essay or problem question was set as part of a course so the obvious starting point is the materials and resources provided by your module tutor; after all, he or she is probably the person who set you the task you are trying to undertake. Go through all the materials that you have collected for that module of your course and, if you have not done so throughout the year, organise your notes.

If, for example, you are required to submit a 2,000 word essay on the concept of the Separation of Powers, the first thing to do is organise and look through your lecture notes and handouts. Read or re-read your tutorial notes on the subject. Your smaller group notes are just as important as those from the large group sessions, because smaller group discussions tend to focus on the topic in a lot more detail and can provide more insight into the problem.

The authors are realists and we are fully aware of the temptations for a student to jump straight to a general Internet search engine, such as Google, as soon as the assessment question hits his or her desk.

Google and similar general purpose Internet search engines are very valuable and powerful search tools. However, they are not designed for legal research and they are insufficiently specific to be efficient in this task. In particular they search the entire Internet, not just legal databases.

As an example, try searching on Google for 'Judicial Review'. At the time of writing, such a search produced: 'About 30,400,000 results (in 0.28 seconds)'.

At first sight it looks very impressive but there are three major problems. First, the sheer volume of material is so huge as to render it unusable. To examine over 30 million Internet references would take many lifetimes. You can look up only the first few.

Second, the material is very wide in its coverage and includes material from almost every English speaking country. Only those from the UK are likely to be of much help (though foreign cases can sometimes be persuasive – see later in this chapter). For example, in the USA, the expression 'Judicial Review' is applied to examination by the Supreme Court of the legality of intended legislation when compared with the US constitution. This is entirely different from the application of the expression in the UK where it refers to the ability of the courts to control administrative actions. The UK courts have no power to alter legislation. Parliament is supreme.

Third, the links provided are not intended for legal research and most are not useful for this purpose. The first few are advertisements offering legal services and the next group are made up of Wikipedia entries and government websites offering advice on how to apply for judicial review. There are then some news articles that happen to have 'Judicial Review' in the headline.

Wikipedia too is an excellent resource but anyone can provide material for it. It is written by the public for the public. The entries rarely provide any identification of their sources. Wikipedia is not an official source and the material it provides can be inaccurate or contradictory. The author of any particular article may have written it from a specific focus on the matter. A decided case may be relevant to more than one area of law. If you are accessing it in relation to one of those areas, but you use an Internet article written by somebody who was writing about a different area, he or she may not have referred to the parts of the decision which are relevant to the area you are researching, and this fact may not be obvious. As a result, you may either dismiss the case outright assuming that it is not relevant, or misinterpret it.

If all you do is search Google and follow the links it provides, you are likely to end up with an infinitesimally small number of the pieces of a very large jigsaw.

If you did so as a practitioner the result would probably be insufficiently specific and dangerously incomplete. As a student, the result is likely to be a sporadic answer that does not provide the full picture in response to the question. Also, your answer is likely to be generic and it will probably not address the question directly. A general Internet search engine will not provide you with the detailed specific data you need to give a structured response to the question and, as a result, your work will fail to analyse the topic at hand.

That is not to say that Google or other general search engines are not useful. They can be used successfully to obtain reports of specific cases and statutes once you have ascertained what the cases and statutes are. However, they are not the best starting point and they most certainly should not be the sole means of research.

By far the best starting point is **Your Course Materials**. Do not forget to check your university's intranet site. Your module leader or course tutor will often have added additional reading lists or materials on the subject page. These are a useful addition to your initial research as are any personal notes from your classes. Once you have gathered your preliminary information, organise it so that it gives you a clear picture.

Often your lecture slides and materials will provide you with a structure to the topic and you would be well advised to use it. They may well also divide the subject into sub topics and this is also likely to be of assistance.

For example, most good lecture notes on the Separation of Powers will include:

(a) A definition of the Separation of Powers doctrine (i.e. very broadly that a modern state is best run if the three arms of government: legislature, executive and judiciary – are kept as separate as possible).

(b) Identification of the relevant organs of government. In the case of the United Kingdom, Parliament, The Civil Service, and the Courts of Law.

(c) Information as to the origins of the doctrine.

(d) Analysis of the extent to which the Separation of Powers is and is not achieved.

(e) A discussion of how the doctrine works within the branches of government.

(f) References to any recent developments in this area of the law; for example, the Constitutional Reform Act 2005.

This is a very good structure for the answer to an essay question.

Having sought out your course materials, including lecture materials and notes from your small group discussions, you should also check your university's online resources for that particular module.

If necessary, re-write or re-type your notes under your proposed structure's sub-topics. You may benefit from either typing these up as a list or creating some form of spider diagram. This will depend upon your learning style. You may find it easier to learn and work with text alone or a more visual aid such as an image or a diagram. For example, a Venn diagram is very useful in relation to the Separation of Powers.

If you reorganise your notes into your identified structure, you will be able, as you progress further into your research, to build on each of your subtopics with your new-found information. If you follow this through to the end of your research you will have a very good collection of notes and a basis for the structure of your essay.

The next source to which you should turn is a **Textbook**. To continue with the Separation of Powers example, the textbook required would probably be one on constitutional law. Read enough of it to identify the doctrine of the Separation of Powers and to understand its basic structure.

It does not matter whether the textbook you use is a physical book or one available electronically, but you do need to read the textbook and you do need to understand the basic structure of the area of law concerned. The main purpose of setting an essay or problem question is to make you do just that.

It is also wise to remember that in most subject areas of law there are two types of textbook, those intended for use by practitioners and those for use by students. The latter tend to concentrate more on describing the law in an understandable way, the former on more detailed description of the state of the law. For this reason it is usually better to start with a student textbook and consult a practitioners' textbook later in the research process. Both will contain references to the cases and statutes which establish the relevant law but the practitioners' textbook will contain far more of such references.

For example, in the law of evidence, one leading students' textbook is *Cross and Tapper on Evidence* (published by Oxford University Press) while the most frequently used practitioner's book is *Phipson On Evidence* (published by Sweet & Maxwell). The practitioners' textbooks are generally larger; they are very much more expensive and well beyond the average student budget. At the time of writing, the current edition of Cross and Tapper is less than £35 while Phipson costs over £300. However, the practitioners' textbooks are likely to be found in any good university law library and many of them are available through online sites to which your university is likely to provide access.

At the start of the year, university students are usually given a module handbook and some recommendations as to the core books on the subject. Unless your budget is severely limited, you should acquire at least one textbook for each study module throughout your university career.

University students are usually also given a recommended reading list and this is a good place to start. The recommendation will include your core textbook but may also refer to a number of other sources which can be found in your university library or accessed online.

Do not feel that you are restricted to the recommended textbook. Student textbooks on the same subject adopt different writing styles and vary in difficulty level so it may be that you do not feel you are getting on well with the core text recommended. If this occurs, discuss it with your tutor and ask if there is another text he or she can recommend. Alternatively, look around the bookshelves in your university library (or check its catalogue, which will probably be available on a computer terminal) or look around the bookshop to find a textbook that suits you better. When you are commencing your studies in a new area it may be that you will benefit from a more basic text which will provide you with the foundation knowledge for the topic and you may then feel ready to progress and deepen your understanding further by moving back to the recommended text.

A very useful alternative to the normal textbooks which will be found in any respectable university law library is *Halsbury's Laws of England* which is published by LexisNexis Butterworths. It is a multi-volume encyclopaedia of the whole of English law and the volumes are frequently republished and brought up to date. Publication of the 5th edition began in 2008 and will consist of just over 100 volumes altogether when completed. It is primarily intended for practitioners and the way it is written is similar to a practitioners' textbook rather than a students' textbook. It is available online as part of the Lexis service and most universities provide their students with access to this resource.

Resist the temptation to dive into the primary sources before you have understood the basic principles. Consulting a judgement at the outset of your research is commendable and certainly preferable to the use of generic secondary Internet sources, but in cases where the facts are complex and the legal principle even more so, you will struggle if you try to go straight to the full text of judgement or an item of legislation before you have completed your preliminary reading.

3. An Explanation of Case Citations

The object of the next stage, research, is to identify the primary sources of law and within those primary sources to find the specific words which relate to the problem in hand. One of the most important of these sources is decided cases.

When cases are referred to in court (the technical term is *cited)* the advocate citing the case is required to give both its name and the reference to where in the Law Reports the case report can be found. It is also almost certain that he or she will wish to quote the words used by the judge or judges which are most relevant to the argument. When this is done the court must be referred to the page of the report where the quotation is to be found.

In the same way, if a professional lawyer is preparing to advise a client he or she will wish to quote the relevant words and should give the relevant law reports reference.

In addition, when a law textbook (or any of the other sources referred to in the section on research) uses a case to illustrate or establish a legal proposition, the textbook will give the case reference. To study law properly it is essential that you read at least the main part of the law report of all the significant cases. To study case law properly you must read what the judge said and this is in the law reports. Only the very briefest extracts appear in the textbooks. You will have seen already that when this book refers to a decided case, the name is followed immediately by the case reference.

In order to find the law report from the reference given in the textbook you need to know what the reference means. It follows that every law student needs, very early in his or her studies, to learn how these references work. Accordingly, a brief explanation follows.

The name of the case is usually the names of the parties separated by the letter **v** and the reference will be in the form:

Somerset v Stewart (1772) 98 ER 499

or **Loveday v Renton** [1990] 1 Med LR 117

As you can see, such a reference breaks down into four components:

(1) The number in brackets is the year in which the report appeared. It is usually the same date or soon after the date when the case was decided.

(2) The next number is the volume of the reports in which the case appears.

(3) The acronym or abbreviation which follows refers to the name of the series of reports. The most often used are:

AC: Appeal Cases. The Official Series law reports of decisions of The House of Lords, the Judicial Committee of the Privy Council and the Supreme Court. The Official Series is published by The Incorporated Council of Law Reporting. The reports contained in this series have been reviewed, before publication, by the judge or judges who tried each case. For this reason the Official Series report should be used in court when available.

AER or All ER: All England Law Reports published by Butterworths.

Ch or ChD: Chancery Division. The Official Series of reports for the Chancery Division and the Court of Appeal hearing appeals in chancery cases.

CrAppR: Criminal Appeal Reports.

ER: English Reports. The Official Series law reports did not appear until 1865. Before that there were only privately published reports available. Often these private series lasted only a very few years. They were usually published only in very small numbers and were often very difficult to obtain. Accordingly a large number of them were reprinted in the English Reports which were published by Stevens & Sons between 1900 and 1932. There are 178 volumes and they reproduce most of the privately published reports of cases from 1220 until 1866.

Fam or FamD: Family Division. The Official Series of reports for the Family Division and the Court of Appeal hearing appeals in family cases.

FLR: Family Law Reports published by Jordan Publishing.

Med LR: Medical Law Reports published by Infirma Law.

QB or QBD: Queen's Bench Division. The Official Series of reports for the Queen's Bench Division of the

High Court and the Court of Appeal hearing appeals in common law civil cases.

WLR: Weekly Law Reports. These are published by the Incorporated Council of Law Reporting. There are three volumes each year. Volume 1 contains the cases which they do not intend to publish in the Official Series. Volumes 2 and 3 contain the reports which are to be published in the Official Series. Because of the need to have the Official Series reports reviewed by the judges, the reports will appear in Volumes 2 and 3 of the WLR much earlier. There is seldom much point in using a report in Volumes 2 or 3 much more than two years old because by then the report will have appeared in the Official Series.

(4) The final number is the page of the report's volume on which the report begins.

If the year is in round brackets, the date is not required in order to find the case, usually because the relevant series of reports is consecutively numbered rather than numbered by reference to the year as, for example, the first citation above which is to the English Reports (see above). The reference to 98 ER is unique even if the date is not stated.

If the date is in square brackets, this is because the year is needed in order to find the report. This is true of most of the modern series of reports. They are numbered, for example, [2010] 1 AER, [2010] 2 AER, [2010] 3 AER and then [2011] 1 AER. Accordingly the volume cannot be identified unless the year is known.

Cases are nowadays often cited by reference to what is called a **neutral citation.** This is a system introduced in 2001. The reference is not to a law report, it is a reference to a transcript of the decision. There is no headnote, no commentary and no reproduction of the arguments presented. These transcripts are available on websites such as Westlaw and students will usually have access to at least one such site. Unfortunately for beginners the neutral citation looks very similar to a law report citation. A neutral citation looks like this:

Kyle Bay Ltd v Underwriters subscribing (to a numbered insurance policy) [2007] EWCA Civ 57.

As you can see it does look very similar to a law report reference. However, the letters and numbers mean different things. The first number is still the date of the publication of the transcript. It is always in square brackets because you cannot find a transcript without the year of publication.

The acronym which follows is not a reference to the law reports series, it refers to the court where the trial was heard. In this case, England and Wales Court of Appeal Civil Division.

The last number is the number of the transcript that year, not a volume or page number. Transcripts under this scheme have numbered paragraphs so internal references are made by using the paragraph numbers. If it is desired to put the paragraph number in the citation it will be added at the end in square brackets.

Once you have been researching for a few weeks you will be able to distinguish very easily which is which. The immediate clues are first that there is no number between the date and the acronym (though this is not conclusive because if a law reports series with its date in square brackets has only enough material for one volume in a particular year, there will be no volume number after the date). Second and most conclusive, there is no series of law reports which uses EWCA as an acronym. Once you get used to the main acronyms you will find it quite easy. EWHC is England and Wales High Court. EWSC is England and Wales Supreme Court.

A full list of the abbreviations of the various law reports series appears in *Halsbury's Laws of England* which can be accessed online by almost all students of Law at recognised UK universities by using the Lexis website. If you navigate to *Halsbury's Laws of England* and to the list of contents, it appears as the first item.

4. Research

The next task is to identify the primary sources of law relevant to the area of investigation. The primary sources of English law are:

(a) Legislation or delegated legislation (Acts of Parliament or Delegated Legislation such as Regulations) and some European Legislation and Regulations

(b) Decided Cases

(c) Immemorial Custom.

While you were reading your university materials or the textbooks it is likely that you encountered references to specific primary sources relevant to each topic area. When you read through your course materials and textbooks you should do so with a sheet of paper and a pen readily to hand and you should note down any such references which appear relevant to the topic you are considering.

You now need to widen the search for primary sources and extend your list of them. Before you do so, review your notes and consider how the information you have gathered could start to come together to form an answer to the relevant question. Identify parts of your structure that require more detail or more emphasis. This will enable you to direct your further research more accurately and, if you have done the job properly up until now, it may very well provide a confidence boost!

For many students, establishing and maintaining motivation can be very difficult especially if the assessment topic area is novel or particularly difficult. However, if you have followed the process for research, outlined in this chapter, by the time you get to the point of expanding your research base you will have achieved an organised set of notes with a structure that is based around the course materials and some further development of these through your module's core text. Having spent the time completing these tasks, you will have made a very good start on the foundations for your assembly, analysis and presentation. This should hopefully spur you to further efforts.

A **Book of Cases and Materials** is a simple, safe and effective method by which to identify and study the main source materials relevant to your topic. Reading it will also enable you better to understand the relevant area of the law, so the next step is to read your book of cases and materials.

Such a book will also provide you with a detailed narrative of the case law and relevant legislation. It will include significant extracts and it will discuss these and their importance to the legal principles established by them. It therefore provides a very good way of bridging the gap between the initial stage of research, and the identification of all the specific primary sources relevant to your subject.

105

The only caveat is that selection of the excerpts and the wording of the narrative are solely dependent upon the author of the book in question. Different authors may place different emphasis upon the differing available primary sources. Like the textbooks, books of cases and materials vary in difficulty and style.

You should not be tempted to miss out the reading of the textbook and go straight to the book of cases and materials. To do so can lead to a lack of full understanding.

If you have not yet read a practitioners' textbook or *Halsbury's Laws of England*, you should do so at this stage. This will increase the list you have of relevant primary sources.

Next, as a student or a practitioner, you will almost certainly have access to **Online Resources**. The relevant statutes and case law can nowadays be found by online searching. This is a very efficient method if done properly but it must be carried out with great care. There are a number of guidelines which it is wise to follow:

(a) What is required is a specifically legal search engine such as Westlaw or Lexis. These are subscription websites and the subscriptions are far from cheap, but a reputable university or college will provide its students with access to one or both of these search engines or else something very similar, and all modern practitioners need such access. It is particularly important to practitioners because for them time is money, and a specifically legal website is several orders of magnitude more efficient than the searching carried out by general search engines.

(b) Such searches are carried out using 'keywords'. In the main it is best to use keywords which are derived from the law not the facts (which is yet another reason for understanding the legal structure first). For instance, if a customer has been sold a defective television, the relevant keywords/phrases are *'sale of goods'* or *'consumer law'* or *'defective product'*, not *'television'*.

(c) If a first search produces disappointing results try using different keywords for the same thing. If the problem concerns a miner who has severe lung disease, a search for *'industrial disease – pneumoconiosis'* might have very different results from a search for *'industrial disease – silicosis'*.

(d) Also check the language of the expression used. Latin phrases are still very common and often produce results radically different from their English equivalents. To give an extreme example, if you search for *'You have the body'* the results will be very different from those of a search for *'Habeas Corpus'*, despite the fact that the English phrase is a direct translation of the Latin one.

107

(e) Expand any truncated words.

(f) If you are searching for more than one specific word try using what are called *'wild cards'* which will search for more than one expression at the same time. For example *'wom*n'* will usually find both occurrences of *'woman'* and *'women'*. A search for *'neligen!'* will usually find any word beginning with those seven letters, *'negligent, negligence, negligently'*. You will need to check the precise wild cards to which the particular website will respond.

(g) Use Boolean variables to link keywords. Boolean expressions are the language of logic. The main Boolean variables are:

AND   NOT   OR
NAND (not and)   NOR (not or)

For example, a search for *'elephant AND clown'* will almost instantaneously locate the case of Behrens v Bertram Mills Circus which is, so far as is known to the authors, the only case in the law reports in which both words appear. (Check which of the Booleans will work; AND, OR and NOT will work on most. The others are much less applicable.)

(h) If your first search produces far too many results, do not abandon it, try refining the search by adding more keywords. For instance, if you enter *'personal injury'* and *'Negligence'* you will get thousands of results. If you add the extra key phrases *'secondary victim'* or *'nervous shock'* or both, you will probably get most of the dozen or so cases which are relevant to those areas.

(i)   Keep a record of the search trail so that you can reproduce it if you need to.

(j)   If you find a relevant case or statutory provision try searching for subsequent references to that case or provision. In that way you should find any later cases or statutory provisions which affect the result you already have.

(k)   When you have identified a relevant case, check the previous authorities which were used or referred to in reaching the decision. Some of them will probably be relevant to your case.

There are many conventional **Dictionaries** available, a leading example being the *Oxford English Dictionary*. This is available online at www.oed.com. Access is too expensive for most student budgets but consult your librarian; your university may have a subscription you can access via your student login.

In addition, if you can afford it, it is worth investing in a legal dictionary. There are a number of these available and you should browse a few of these at the bookshop to see which suits you best.

Yet again, resist the temptation to use a general Internet search engine. Doing so or seeking out a free legal online dictionary will certainly find you a definition but it is likely to provide you with no more than a few very basic terms and definitions, most of which can be found in the glossary of your student textbook. For example, the range of words beginning with 'G' provided by some online legal dictionaries runs to only six words, whereas a proper legal dictionary will provide a much more extensive range.

The eagle-eyed amongst you may have noted that the authors have not yet referred to **Revision Guides**. Their omission until now is not because we wished to 'leave the best to last'. We simply do not recommend their use for legal research purposes, certainly not as the sole text consulted. Despite their approachable colourful pages and their lightweight attributes, they are exactly what they describe themselves to be – revision guides. They are not full textbooks, they tend to be in note form and they do not usually elaborate upon or discuss the topics in any detail. They are intended to refresh your memory in relation to topics you have already learned; they are no substitute for a fully worded textbook in the learning or research process. They can also be used to check that you have identified all the basic topics that should be covered within a specific area of law.

There are almost certain to be a number of **Journal Articles** which contain relevant material. Practitioners invariably have online access to these and most universities provide students with access to them.

Check with your librarian as to which databases are available to you.

Journal articles often provide a very useful source of narrative and critique of the law. Many journals are the result of ongoing academic research and as they do not need to undergo the same lengthy publication process as textbooks, they are usually much more up to date.

As you read through all this material you should continue to keep notes of all the relevant primary sources to which you have referred. When you have completed the process you should have a full list of the relevant primary sources and if you followed the advice to devise a structure first, it should be in a reasonably suitable order.

Having assembled a list of the primary sources, the next step is to obtain and read them and make sure that you understand the effect of each case decision and each statutory provision.

There are two golden rules to this stage of the process. First, obtain the text of each primary source of law from an appropriate source of such material. Second, read all of it.

Whether you use books or online sources does not matter but the quality of the sources you use certainly does. For cases use the Law Reports where the text of the judgement will be given in full and the effect of the decision fully summarised in the headnote. For

Legislation or Delegated Legislation use official sources or volumes or online sources which contain verbatim recitals of the material, not summaries. (Statutes and delegated legislation are often amended so make very sure you have the most up-to-date edition.) The UK Government's own website: **www.legislation.gov.uk** is an outstandingly good source because the legislation appears with tracked changes. As a result, its current state at any particular date can be obtained quite easily and even proposed changes which are not yet in force are in the notes.

As you read the material you should look for the specific parts of it that contain the core of the decision or legislative provision which relates to your specific case or question.

By way of example, take a claim in negligence for damages for personal injuries where the victim was not directly injured by the act of negligence but suffered a psychological injury as a result of witnessing what happened to someone else. Such a person is usually called a 'secondary victim'. A leading example arose from the Hillsborough Disaster because many relatives of the primary victims brought claims for damages for Post-Traumatic Stress Disorder caused by seeing what happened to members of their families on television.

Such claims are heavily restricted on policy grounds. Let us suppose that as a student you are asked to write an essay on the topic: 'What restrictions are placed by the law on the recovery of compensation for personal injury by secondary victims and why?'

First, note again that exactly the same process would be required if it were a problem question or a mooting problem giving the facts of a secondary victim case or if you were a practitioner with a client who wished to bring such a claim or even a judge trying to write a judgement in such a case.

You would have begun by identifying the relevant areas of law as the Tort of Negligence, the recovery of damages for personal injuries, nervous shock and specifically secondary victims. The relevant reference in *Halsbury's Laws* is: 5th edition (2010), Volume 78 paragraph 12 'Liability for Psychiatric Damage, Nervous shock'.

Your research thus far should have identified about 10 to 15 cases including **McLoughlin v O'Brian** [1983] AC 410. The relevant law is all in decided cases; there are no significant statutory provisions.

Before you begin reading the reports, assemble them in date order and read them in sequence. As you do so, you should note that in the speech of Lord Wilberforce in the **McLoughlin** case (at p. 421 of the report) he said:

'there remains, in my opinion, just because "shock" in its nature is capable of affecting so wide a range of people, a real need for the law to place some limitation upon the extent of admissible claims. It is necessary to consider three elements

inherent in any claim: the class of persons whose claim should be recognised: the proximity of such persons to the accident: and the means by which shock is caused.'

Hopefully, you will realise as you read it that this is highly relevant to the essay and that it is the beginning of an encapsulation of the law on the subject. You should make a note of what Lord Wilberforce said and where in the report the specific words are to be found. If you then continue this process through the remainder of this case and all the other cases in your list, identifying the key passages and recording what they say and where they are to be found you will hopefully:

(a) Identify the restrictions placed on the ability of secondary victims to recover.

(b) Identify the reasons for those restrictions.

(c) Be able to give the references to and to quote the judgements which support those restrictions and the reasons for them.

You have now obtained the primary source material you need to write the essay, to answer the problem question, to advise the client or to argue the case before a court or at a moot.

However, make sure that you have run each of your 10 to 15 cases through some form of search for any subsequent reference. (For this purpose a search on Lexis, Westlaw or some similar legal research website is much the quickest and most effective way.) That will ensure that your primary sources are fully up to date.

You may wish to include material you have found which is not directly derived from primary sources but which is nonetheless persuasive. There are a number of possibilities:

First, the decisions of courts in other jurisdictions. The decisions of the European Court of Human Rights in Strasbourg and those of the Court of the European Community in Luxembourg do have direct authority in the law of England and Wales. Most other non-domestic decisions are not authoritative but they can be used to persuade. This is particularly true of cases from the Commonwealth countries because most of them have Common Law Systems and their rules therefore tend to be similar to our own. Make sure, however, that their rules on the particular topic in question are parallel to our own before you use such a case.

Second, there are many decisions by courts in the United Kingdom which are not authoritative. This fact should be borne in mind when compiling your list of primary sources. There is a practice note dealing with this which was issued by Lord Woolf CJ on 8 April 2001. You will find it at [2001] 2 AER 510. It gives details of cases which should not be cited as authority. You should obtain and read it. Broadly speaking, decisions of the County Court are not authoritative and neither are decisions of the higher courts taken in circumstances where only one party was present or where the only decision taken was whether the case was arguable rather than whether it was right (such as the grant of permission to appeal or the grant of permission to begin proceedings for judicial review).

However, if you can find such a decision on facts very closely similar to those with which you are dealing, it can be used persuasively. It would be wise to use such a citation with some caution if addressing the Court of Appeal or the Supreme Court, but it could certainly be done in a case at first instance or in a moot or a mock trial.

Third, statements of opinion made by academic lawyers, the authors of journal articles or the authors of textbooks are not authoritative primary sources of the Law of England and Wales, but they too can be used persuasively both in written work and in oral presentations in court, so if you encounter a particularly cogent phrase or paragraph in a textbook do not hesitate to quote it.

Fourth, not everything said by a judge in the course of giving judgement is necessarily authoritative. Utterances by judges during judgements are divided between:

(i) Those comments which are required in order to support the decision. These are authoritative and (despite recent attempts to abandon the use of Latin in the law) are still referred to using the Latin expression 'Ratio Decidendi' and

(ii) Those comments made as asides which are not essential to the decision. These are not authoritative. They are usually referred to as 'Obiter Dicta' (or just 'obiter'). Although these are not authoritative, they can be used persuasively.

You should also note that occasionally a decision is taken by one of the senior courts which is contradicted by a binding previous authority. This can happen if the parties' advocates fail to tell the court that the previous authority exists and as a result it is not referred to in the course of argument. Such decisions are referred to as having been taken 'Per Incuriam' and their authority can be challenged on this ground.

5. Assembly and Analysis

Having obtained all the relevant material the next stage is to assemble it in an appropriate order and to analyse and summarise what it says as to the state of the law. The order in which you assemble it will depend entirely on the nature of the problem and the context in which it is set. The nature of the analysis will also be entirely dependent on the nature of the required outcome.

If the outcome is to be an essay, an order which is either chronological or thematic will probably be best, and the analysis will consist of examination of the background and history and the expression of some sort of view as to the present state of the law based on the authorities which the research has identified. Where it is definite, state what it is and cite the primary source. Where it is uncertain, explain that this is the case and why, and again quote the relevant primary sources.

If the outcome is the answer to a problem question then answer the question to the best of your ability, given the state of the law as it appears from the authorities. Explain the answer and justify each point by reference to the authorities. Again, if the law is uncertain, say so, say why and cite the authorities.

If you have to advise a client (whether face to face in conference or in a written opinion) again you need to answer the question, which will usually be: *'Will my claim (or my defence to this claim) succeed?'* You must answer this question to the best of your ability given the state of the law as it appears from the authorities. Again explain the answer and justify each point by reference to the authorities.

In most cases the outcome of the case will depend both on factual/evidential and legal issues and both need to be analysed and the results presented to the client. This ties in with stage 6 in Chapter 3.

There is no significant difference between the assembly and analysis required for presentation to a court and that required for presentation in a mock trial or a moot. This is because both moots and mock trials are designed to reproduce, as closely as possible in a student context, the conditions in a real courtroom.

In each case what is required is a logical structure which presents the arguments in favour of your case. The structure is likely to be thematic. Your second point may depend on establishing your first, your third on establishing your second, and so on. Your assembly and analysis needs to construct the argument in a logical step-by-step manner supporting each step in the process with reference to authority, either something said in the course of a judgement or something contained in a statutory provision or in delegated legislation. In default of clear authority you can use persuasive material, or you can use persuasive material in support of an authority, but as far as possible back up every stage in the process by reference to at least one authority of some kind.

Do not simply cite one authority for each proposition. If you have several clear authorities for any given proposition use all of them (unless the numbers are so large that this becomes impractical, which will be a very rare occurrence). An old saying among rock climbers is *'never use one belay where six will do'* and much the same philosophy applies to authorities in a legal argument.

6. Addressing and Referring to Judges

The only task remaining is presentation and this is dealt with in the next section but, before we pass on to that stage, there are some largely unwritten rules and conventions about referring to, addressing and writing about judges which all students need to know.

First, **addressing a judge in court**. Judges of the Supreme Court, the Court of Appeal and the High Court are all addressed as '*My Lord*' or '*My Lady*' or '*Your Lordship*' or '*Your Ladyship*'.

Circuit Judges are addressed as '*Your Honour*' which is gender neutral. There are two exceptions. First some Circuit Judges sit occasionally as judges of the High Court. When they do so they are addressed as judges of the High Court. Second, some Circuit Judges have been given the honorary title of '*Recorder of* (a City)'. When they sit in that capacity they are addressed as if they were judges of the High Court.

District Judges either in the County Court or the Magistrates' Court are addressed as '*Sir*' or '*Madam*'. A lay (that is non-legally qualified) magistrate is addressed as '*Your Worship*'. Again this is gender neutral. Since lay magistrates commonly sit in benches of two to seven, the plural form '*Your Worships*' is more commonly heard.

Second, **writing about judges**. The holders of high judicial posts are very often referred to in writing by using abbreviations. The Lord Chief Justice of England and Wales is often referred to in writing by his title and name (or her title and name, though in England and Wales the office has not yet been held by a woman) followed by the letters CJ. There is an example in Rule 10 of Chapter 1 of this book where there is reference to Lord Mansfield CJ. The more condensed form of the name followed by the letters LCJ is sometimes seen but should not now be used. The Master of the Rolls is referred to by his/her title and name followed by the letters MR. The President of the Family Division is referred to by his/her title and name followed by the letter P. Judges of the Supreme Court are referred to as *'Lord'* or *'Lady'* followed by the name and then the letters SCJ which is short for *'Supreme Court Justice'*. The President and Deputy President of the Supreme Court have the Letters P and DP immediately after the name and before the SCJ. Formerly, members of the Judicial House of Lords were referred to simply as *'Lord'* or *'Lady'* or sometimes *'Baron'* or *'Baroness'* followed by the name. There is, in their case, no commonly used abbreviation. Judges of the Court of Appeal are referred to by their name followed by the letters LJ which is gender neutral because it can be short for *'Lord Justice'* or *'Lady Justice'*. Judges of the High Court are referred to by the name followed by the single letter J which is short for *'Mr Justice'* or *'Mrs Justice'* or *'Ms Justice'* as appropriate.

Note that, thus far, the abbreviation follows the name. For a Circuit Judge or a District Judge the practice changes. A Circuit Judge is referred to using the letters HHJ which is short for *'His Honour Judge'* or *'Her Honour Judge'* followed by the name. Sometimes just the HH is abbreviated and the *'Judge'* appears in full. A District Judge is referred to using the letters DJ followed by the name.

With magistrates the order reverts. A magistrate is formally referred to as a *'Justice of the Peace'* so the short form is the name followed by the letters JP.

The use of the given names of judges follows the practice applied to children in the age of Jane Austen. The first daughter of the Bennett family (Jane) was *'Miss Bennett'*. Second and subsequent daughters were given their first names as in *'Miss Elizabeth Bennett'*. So the first person called Kay (his given name was John) to become a High Court Judge in recent years was referred to as *'Mr Justice Kay'* or in writing *'Kay J'*. The second was referred to as *'Mr Justice Maurice Kay'* or in writing *'Maurice Kay J'*.

Finally, **speaking about judges**. The abbreviated form should never be used orally in court or in any other formal setting. Even if you are reading from a document, such as a law report, which contains an abbreviated form you should not speak in the abbreviated form. You should use the full form. You read *'Waterhouse J'*. You say *'Mr Justice Waterhouse'*. You read *'Lord Mansfield CJ'*. You say either *'The Lord Chief Justice, Lord Mansfield'* or *'Lord Chief Justice Mansfield'*. When referring orally to judges of the Supreme Court, just say *'Lord'* or *'Lady'* followed by the name. Do not repeat either the abbreviation SCJ, or its expansion.

In addition, if you read a reference to a judge in a report published before he or she was appointed to a higher court it is customary to read the name as it appears in the report, though with any abbreviation expanded, and then add *'as he/she then was'*.

7. Presentation

If your presentation is a coursework essay or the answer to a coursework problem question, all you need to do now is to write out the results of your assembly and analysis and hand it in.

Preferably, do not leave the write-up and hand-in until the last minute. As already stated, the authors are realists and are well aware that on many occasions deadlines are very close or even have been exceeded before the work is completed. It is accepted that this is an inevitable part of student life. However, frantic activity at the last minute is scarcely likely to lead to high-quality results.

The pressure of a looming deadline, no structure, just lots of random excerpts of material and a lonely cursor flashing at you from a very blank screen, can all lead to a horrible quagmire of assessment stress. The outcome may well be that you work until 4 a.m. of the day of the deadline fortified by coffee or some other caffeine-laced drink and eventually reach the stage where you will hand in almost anything. You will probably wake up after a sleep which was far too short and realise that your paper still needs a lot of work.

Working under such pressure with no direction is not normally productive and the more the deadline looms the worse the panic gets and clear and constructive thought becomes ever more difficult. The Law of the Cussedness of Inanimate Objects (alias Murphy's Law) being what it is, your computer printer will inevitably choose just this moment to cease to function properly.

When you do finally submit your work, the likelihood is that you will know it is not your best effort and you will feel exhausted and more than a little disappointed. University is hard enough without putting yourself under so much pressure.

You can avoid involvement in this nightmare if you start work soon after the assignment is set, if you take the time at the start of your assessment to work on the preliminary steps to research and identify your structure and required topics for discussion and if you continue to apply yourself to the task on a regular basis throughout the period of time available to you. This applies to both essays and problem questions.

If your presentation is to be advice to a client either in writing or in a face-to-face conference, again your task is more or less complete at the assembly and analysis stage. All you need to do is write the advice in line with that assembly and analysis. Even if the advice to the client is to be given orally, it is good practice to write out at least a brief note containing the basic structure, the results of the analysis and the list of authorities. This can then be used as notes at the conference and, if appropriate, given to the client after the conference so that the client has an adequate aide-memoire as to what has been said.

How to Create a Legal Argument

If the presentation is to be an oral submission in a court, moot or mock trial the structure and content of the argument have been completed but a little more needs to be said on the subject of presentation.

Primarily what is required is a step-by-step methodical explanation of the case being put forward supporting each proposition in turn by reference to authority and/or persuasive material.

Do bear in mind what was said in the first chapter of this book about speaking in public. There is little place for the techniques of rhetoric in a legal argument. Its strength is in its logic and in the weight and relevance of the authorities cited. The tribunal may enjoy it more if it is expressed with great oratorical brilliance but it will be no more likely to succeed than if it had been delivered in a monotone. However, the basic rules of public speaking remain relevant. Talk to your tribunal not at them. Maintain eye contact. If you are advancing a complex stage-by-stage argument, make sure the judge or judges understand (and hopefully accept) step one before you move on to step two. If they fail to understand on the first occasion try a different way of explaining the same proposition.

If you are arguing a particularly difficult or complex problem, try to present the court with an appropriate analogy.

Speak slowly and clearly. In a real courtroom you should never rush at all. The time limits imposed upon students in moots and mock trials sometimes lead participants to speak very quickly indeed in order to 'get in' as much material as they can on the basis that they will gain more marks from the inclusion of the additional material than they will lose as a result of speaking too fast. Regrettably this analysis is on some occasions correct. This is unfortunate because the purpose of mooting and mock trials is to train students in the skills and techniques of courtroom advocacy and giving them an incentive to gabble is most definitely counter-productive.

The constraints of mooting time limits make it difficult to give firm advice on the subject but a balance has to be struck between lack of material as a result of shortage of time and lack of coherence as a result of speaking too fast. Certainly it is very unwise to speak so fast that your tribunal is unable to follow what you are saying.

If you are presenting a legal argument to one of the higher courts, you need to bear in mind the rules about the citation of authorities. These govern which series of law reports should be used when decided cases are quoted and how the copies should be provided for use by the court. You will find the rules at: Practice Direction (Citation of Authorities) [2012] 1 WLR 780.

The practice direction itself states that it applies to the Senior Courts of England and Wales including the Crown Court and in County Courts and Magistrates Courts but, despite what it says, in cases at first instance in the County Court, the Crown Court, the Magistrates Court and even the High Court in some circumstances, the citation rules are honoured more in the breach than in the observance. Judges in provincial County Courts are generally content to have whatever report of a decided case is available and will scarcely ever complain that the wrong report has been provided. In the higher courts the rules are very strictly applied and should be obeyed rigorously.

Next there are three 'golden rules' which should never under any circumstances be broken. First, **never take a bad point**, that is one which you know is unsound or so weak as not to be worth arguing. Taking a bad point is certain to alienate the judge.

Second, if your argument contains a number of propositions of varying strengths, **put your best point first** and continue in descending order. There can have been few more withering comments from the bench than one addressed by Lord Widgery CJ to a member of the bar who had been on his feet arguing his case for about 40 minutes when His Lordship said ' *I know Mr xxxxx, you are saving your best point until last aren't you?'*

Third, **you must tell the court of any contradictory authority**. If your research discloses a decided case or statutory provision which contradicts your argument tell the court that it exists and give the reference to it. To fail to do so is a serious breach of your ethical responsibilities. To fail to find it is negligent. To find it and fail to disclose it is dishonest.

Advocacy and Public Speaking

You may also need, in a presentation to a court, a moot or a mock trial, to refute a legal argument put forward by the opposition. This may be done:

(a) by attacking the appropriateness or accuracy of their summary of the decided cases or their analysis of what the cases say.

(b) by attacking the authority of the cases they rely upon, for instance they may rely on an authority which was decided per incuriam or one which is listed in the 2001 practice note as being a case which ought not be cited as authority.

(c) by pointing out that there is a subsequent case which overrules one or more of the authorities they are relying on.

(d) by referring to authorities which contradict the propositions which they put forward.

The authors strongly recommend that as law students you should take part in moots and mock trials whenever you can. One of the main foundations for success both during your degree and beyond is to become proficient in public speaking, including legal argument. Until we discover how to move the Felix Felicis Potion from the world of Harry Potter into reality, the only way to improve on your ability to construct and present a successful legal argument is to practise. Moots and mock trials have their limitations but they are very good practice.

CHAPTER 5

HOW TO DRAFT A SKELETON ARGUMENT

*And he said unto me: Prophesy upon these bones and say
unto them: O ye dry bones, hear the word of the Lord.
Thus saith the Lord God unto these bones: Behold I will
cause breath to enter into you and ye shall live; and I will
lay sinews upon you and will bring up flesh upon you and
cover you with skin and put breath in you and ye shall live.*
Ezekiel 37:3–5

*Skeletons ... are the tools of persuasion ... Your skeleton is
your chance to tell the Judge what the case is about, what
you want and why you should have it in no more
than the time between the judicial supper and bed;
much less if possible. If you get it wrong and the
other side get it right, they are already ahead.*
HH Nicholas Chambers QC
Case Handling, an Illustrated View from the Bench

1. Introduction

During your time at university you are likely on
occasions to be required to prepare skeleton
arguments. A skeleton argument is always required
when you are preparing for a moot. The requirement
will reoccur when you become a practitioner, especially
in cases where there is to be a legal argument.

This chapter will take you through the purpose and
definition of a skeleton argument and how you should
construct and structure your document. The ability to

develop an effective skeleton argument is becoming more and more important at undergraduate level. Many universities are now placing much more emphasis on their students developing practical legal skills. Furthermore, these skills are often regarded as part of a student's ongoing progression and are assessed.

Mooting, with the inclusion of drafting a skeleton argument, is a task that lends itself very well to an assessment project. Even if your course does not impose such a requirement, the authors would still suggest strongly that you should take part in mooting and recommend that you seek out opportunities to represent your university, in one or more of the large number of national and regional mooting competitions that take place each year. Whether your moot is subject to an assessment criterion or delivered as part of a competition, it is almost certain that you will be required to draft a skeleton argument. Developing this skill now will benefit you tremendously in your later career, both on the vocational courses and in practice.

2. Definition and Purpose

A skeleton argument is a short written document that is placed before a court in advance of a trial or an oral hearing in order to set out in advance the main structure of the case to be advanced on behalf of a party. It is intended to outline the main points of a party's case and is drafted by his or her advocate.

It is called a skeleton argument because it is intended to encapsulate in very brief form the basic structure of the argument. The term provides its own definition. It is intended to contain the 'bare bones' of your intended oral submissions and you will be well advised always to remember this when writing a skeleton argument. It should consist of the main points/the foundations of your client's case. You will build on it and apply the flesh and sinews (as the Lord said he would do in the Ezekiel quotation) when you come to present the case in the oral hearing.

Acquiring and maintaining the ability to construct a succinct yet persuasive skeleton argument, which demonstrates both your main points in a case and the authorities to be relied upon, is a skill vital to any advocate. PD52A section 5 of The Civil Procedure Rules governs the presentation of skeleton arguments in appeals in civil proceedings. Strictly, it does not apply to other cases, but the principles set out in it are universally applicable and you should consult it in every case. Its text is as follows:

'SECTION V – SKELETON ARGUMENTS
5.1

(1) The purpose of a skeleton argument is to assist the court by setting out as concisely as practicable the arguments upon which a party intends to rely.

(2) A skeleton argument must –

- *be concise;*
- *both define and confine the areas of controversy;*
- *be set out in numbered paragraphs;*
- *be cross-referenced to any relevant document in the bundle;*
- *be self-contained and not incorporate by reference material from previous skeleton arguments;*
- *not include extensive quotations from documents or authorities.*

(3) Documents to be relied on must be identified.

(4) Where it is necessary to refer to an authority, a skeleton argument must –

- *(a) state the proposition of law the authority demonstrates; and*
- *(b) identify the parts of the authority that support the proposition.*

If more than one authority is cited in support of a given proposition, the skeleton argument must briefly state why.'

3. Content and Structure

As you have seen, CPR PD52A paragraph 5.1 gives clear guidance on the content and structure of a skeleton argument. You will notice the PD is neither strongly prescriptive nor excessively proscriptive. This ensures that the individual drafting style of the advocate is permitted some leeway, and in addition, the format of a skeleton argument needs to be sufficiently flexible to be capable of encompassing a wide array of cases.

You will see also that there is an emphasis upon keeping the skeleton argument as succinct as possible. A skeleton should be skeletal. An obese skeleton is a contradiction in terms both in reality and metaphorically. **KISS** applies even more here than it does in public speaking.

It might be expected that everyone would readily understand from the use of the term skeleton that brevity is required. Regrettably this is far from universally the case. Among both practitioners and students in mooting competitions, the temptation to develop a more substantial argument, one that flexes muscles and is seen sporting the latest apparel, is all too common. When composing a skeleton argument make sure you have a brightly coloured Post-it® note stuck to the side of your screen, with the word 'skeleton' written upon it. This will hopefully serve as a reminder and steer you away from inadvertently writing the advocate's version of *War and Peace*.

4. Drafting

Begin with a very short summary of the facts of the case. A skeleton argument needs to be self-contained and a recital of the facts is essential, but keep it as short as possible consistent with including all the essential facts. It should rarely be more than half a page.

If there is a dispute about any of the facts, say so, say what your case is in relation to the disputed facts, list the evidence and law upon which you propose to rely in support of your case and why you say it should be persuasive.

If there is a dispute about the law, which will be by far the most common reason why a skeleton argument is required, set out again as briefly as possible what your case on the law is, list the authorities you rely on in support and quote very briefly the statutory provisions or the sections from the judgements which encapsulate the propositions on which you rely. When you did your legal research (see Chapter 4) and analysed your results you produced a summary of the state of the law on the relevant subject with a list of the primary sources and quotations from them and a list of persuasive material with quotations from it.

You should use this material to draft a skeleton argument. Set out what you say the law is in a series of short direct propositions and support each with a list of the authorities relevant to it. CPR PD 52A does say that if you cite more than one authority for each proposition you should say why you have done so. This is honoured more in the breach than the observance.

The reason is that in most practical circumstances the skeleton argument does double duty as a list of the authorities on which it is intended to rely in the oral presentation of the argument. Only in the highest courts is such a list submitted separately. So if there are five authorities in support of a given proposition say there are five and list them. As a reason, just say they are all necessary to establish the point. Unless you really need to, do not quote from any of them. Just state the proposition and list the cases as supporting it but do list all of them unless the number really is very large indeed, in which case you would probably be better advised to stick to the most important half-dozen even in the course of the oral presentation.

Having said that, if you have one authority which is of great weight such as a decision of the House of Lords or the new Supreme Court and your other authorities are of less weight, you need refer in a skeleton argument only to the heavyweight case unless the other cases add some important clarification.

Above all, keep it short. The object of the exercise is to encapsulate the essential core of your argument in as brief a form as possible. Remember that you are not trying to write out in full the entire text of your subsequent oral presentation. In a real court case, unless the case is very complex indeed, if a skeleton argument exceeds five or six pages of A4 typescript there is something seriously wrong. In moots or mock trials the limit placed upon their length is usually very much less than that. You need to acquire and apply the skill of encapsulating what you intend to say in as few words as possible.

Finally, submit your skeleton argument in good time. Directions commonly require skeleton arguments two to four days before the hearing. In the higher courts failure to do this is rare (because the consequences are severe) but at lower levels all too commonly advocates hand them in to the court clerk on the morning of the hearing, sometimes five or 10 minutes before the case begins. This may or may not draw a judicial rebuke but even if it does not, if yours is one case in a list of several, the judge simply will not be able to read it properly; either he or she will just skim through it, in which case you will probably have wasted your time or, if he or she does read it properly, you will delay the court. In addition, he or she will probably have spent some time (often many hours) reading the trial documents in advance. This process is considerably helped (and hence shortened) if he or she has read the skeleton argument **before** reading the rest of the trial bundle. If the judge has completed the process without this help, and is then given the skeleton argument when there is no time to read it properly, this is scarcely likely to improve your reputation as an advocate.

CHAPTER 6

EXAMINING, CROSS-EXAMINING AND
RE-EXAMINING WITNESSES

Cross-examination is the greatest legal engine ever invented for the discovery of truth. You can do anything with a bayonet except sit on it. A lawyer can do anything with cross-examination if he is skillful enough not to impale his own cause upon it.

John Henry Wigmore

1. Introduction

When a witness is called to give evidence to a court, he or she is first asked questions by the advocate acting for the party who called the witness. This is called 'examination-in-chief' or 'direct examination'. Then he or she is asked questions by the advocate(s) for the opposing party (or parties). This is referred to as 'cross-examination'. Finally, the advocate for the party who called the witness is permitted to ask any questions arising from the cross-examination. This is called 're-examination'.

Remember Chapter 3, which advised that when preparing the case you should start at the end and work towards the beginning (Reverse Planning)? Preparing either the examination-in-chief or the cross-examination of each witness is merely a continuation of this process. Remember:

(A) Question 3 in Chapter 3, part 7 (p. 70):

Q3: (a) To what extent do I already have this material?

    (b) To the extent that I do already have this material, where is it?

    (c) To the extent that I do not have this material, can I get it and, if so, where and how?

    (d) How am I going to make sure that this material is properly before the court by the end of the hearing?

(B) Part 11 of Chapter 3, 'Presentation' (p. 83).

(C) Question 4 in Chapter 3, part 10 (p. 78):

Q4: What parts of my opponent's evidence do I need to refute/challenge and how do I go about it?

This is now the stage at which you put the material before the court. To the extent that you have evidence in support of your own case (Q3) or evidence to contradict the opposing case (the first two headings following Q4 in Chapter 3, part 10), you will need to call the witnesses and/or produce the exhibits. This is dealt with in examination-in-chief.

The other three headings following Q4 in Chapter 3, part 10 are matters for cross-examination. In either case you have come to the next question in the 'start at the back' sequence. Take each witness in turn and, in planning your examination-in-chief or your cross-examination, ask yourself:

Q5:

(a) What am I trying to achieve with this witness?
(b) How am I going to achieve it?

2. Examination-in-Chief

In civil cases in England and Wales other than the rare cases which involve civil juries, it is now customary, instead of a normal examination-in-chief, for the judge to read the witness statements in advance of the trial and for counsel calling a witness at the trial simply to have the witness confirm the accuracy of the witness statement and to ask a very few supplemental questions. However, in criminal and many family cases, the process usually involves taking the witness through the evidence orally.

It is in general terms forbidden, in examination-in-chief, to ask what is called a 'leading question'. A leading question is one which suggests the answer the witness is to give. For example: '*the car which caused the accident was red wasn't it?*' is a leading question, but '*What colour was the car?*' is not. A leading question is sometimes referred to as a 'closed' question. A question which is not leading is sometimes referred to as 'open'.

The expression 'leading question' is sometimes defined as a question which can be answered either 'yes' or 'no' but this is not an adequate definition. Not all questions so answerable are leading and many questions which are leading cannot be so answered. Moreover, whether a question is leading or not may depend on the circumstances. If a witness has already said that the car which caused the accident '*was either green or blue, I am not sure which*', it would not be a leading question to ask: '*Was the car green or was it blue?*' If the colour had not been previously specified, this would be a leading question. Note that in either circumstance the question cannot, in practical terms, be answered 'yes' or 'no'.

Usually, where the circumstances permit only two possibilities, it is not a leading question to ask which is correct. If a witness has already said he was standing on the station platform when the train came in, it is not leading to ask '*Did you get on the train*?' because there are only two possible answers and the question does not suggest which answer the questioner wants. It would still be leading to say '*You did get on the train didn't you*?'

There are no hard and fast rules about examination-in-chief. The general answer to question 5 (a) is that the objective is to get the witness to give the necessary evidence – usually to tell the court what happened. As to question 5 (b), what is required is a series of non-leading questions which guide or prompt the witness to tell the story.

The basic guidelines are:

(1) Always remember that, of the cases you win, the vast majority will be won by the evidence you call in support of your case rather than by damage done to your opponent's case in cross-examination. Evidence in chief is very important.

(2) As in every other area of practice, be very thoroughly prepared. Plan in advance what you

want the witness to say and in what order. A logical order is essential. It will usually, but not invariably, be chronological. It is as well to make a written note of the facts about which you wish the witness to give evidence and to tick them off (either physically or mentally) as the evidence proceeds. The appropriate order should have been taken into account when the witness statement was drafted, in which case you should be able to work from the witness statement and any extra notes you need can be written in the margin on your copy. If the witness statement is not in the order you want, more detailed notes may be required. When the witness has given evidence of all the items you need, stop. NEVER continue into material you do not need, particularly when you do not know what the witness is going to say.

(3) Tell each witness at the outset that although you will be asking the questions, they should face the judge or the jury. There are two reasons for this: first you want the witnesses to communicate with the tribunal of fact and for that, eye contact is important. Second, you will often be much closer to the witnesses than the judge or the jury and even more often you will be in a completely different direction as viewed from the witness box. If the witnesses face you they will subconsciously pitch their voices to you and it may be difficult for the judge or jury to hear. A judge who cannot hear can be expected to say so, a juror may well be reluctant

to interrupt. If, as a result, some or all of the jurors have not heard the evidence then the intended effect of the evidence may not have been achieved. If the witnesses look at the judge or jury they will usually pitch their voices at a level audible to the judge or jury. This is particularly important in courts without amplification and it is a surprising fact in the 21st century that there are many courts which are still without amplification.

(4) Keep control of the evidence. Do direct the witness to the areas of evidence you want: *'can you give us a description of the man responsible? How tall would you say he was?'* – but once you have done so, leave it to the witness.

(5) Let the witness tell the story. The judge or the jury want the evidence from the witness, not from the advocate.

(6) Be prepared to prevent the witness (firmly, if necessary, but always politely) from deviating into irrelevancies, or even more important, into inadmissible material, especially when prosecuting in a jury case.

(7) If the witness is giving the evidence relatively well, just prompt when required using short, simple questions such as: *'What happened then?'* though avoid using the same prompt each time.

There are two areas in which major problems can arise with evidence in chief:

(a) The witness who must be prevented from giving evidence you do not want him or her to give.

(b) Cases where it is very difficult to get the witness to give the evidence.

In the former category are cases where the witness statement contains material which is either not admissible in evidence or which for other reasons you do not wish the witness to give. This will arise most often when you prosecute in criminal cases and examples are hearsay and evidence that the defendant has a previous criminal record.

Hearsay is evidence of fact which the witness has not perceived himself or herself but which he or she has been told about by somebody else. At one time there was a near total prohibition of the use of hearsay evidence in both civil and criminal cases. Now, subject to rules of court, it is generally admissible in civil cases but there are still significant restrictions on its use in criminal cases (although there are now many circumstances in which it can be admitted).

That a defendant in a criminal case has previous convictions can nowadays sometimes be put in evidence by the prosecution with the leave of the court but nevertheless the general rule is that such material is not admissible evidence.

Witnesses must if necessary be prevented from giving any inadmissible evidence. This is particularly important when prosecuting in the Crown Court where the trial is by jury because if a witness is permitted to blurt out something inadmissible which is prejudicial to the defendant it may well be necessary to discharge the jury and start the trial again. If this has resulted from a careless question or a careless failure to realise that the witness is going to say something inadmissible, the advocate may very well be blamed for the need for a retrial. Certainly if you are undertaking your training as a solicitor or barrister and you make this kind of mistake you are likely to fail the relevant module.

If the problem is apparent on the face of the witness statements it is easy enough to deal with. You simply need to preface your questions appropriately, for example:

'Mr Smith, I would like you to tell the court what happened in the incident. It is very important that you describe only what you yourself saw and heard. Please do not refer to anything which you did not see or hear but which you were told by anybody else.'

or:

'Mrs Jones, it is very important that you confine your evidence to what happened on this particular day. Please do not refer to events from any other incident, just stick to the matter in hand.'

It is much more difficult to control a witness who suddenly blurts out additional and inadmissible material which is not in his or her witness statement, but if you are fortunate enough to spot in advance that this is going to happen you must intervene in some way, for example:

'Mrs Blenkinsop, I apologise for interrupting you but it rather sounded as though you were about to tell us something which does not relate to the matters in hand. Please remember to confine your evidence to what happened that day. Do not refer to anything else.'

A witness in the second category usually falls into one of three subgroups:

(a) The witness, often a child or a rape victim, who is so overwhelmed by the occasion that they remain silent.

(b) The witness who for whatever reason has changed his or her mind about giving evidence (often a woman who has been assaulted by her husband or partner but who has subsequently been reconciled with him). Such a witness is often referred to as a **reluctant witness**.

(c) The witness who gives evidence contradicting what is in the witness statement. Such a witness is usually referred to as a **hostile witness**.

The evidence in chief of children (and sometimes other vulnerable witnesses) is usually provided by way of a pre-recorded video interview which is simply played in court. Nevertheless, examination-in-chief of such a witness, sometimes by CCTV, may still be required in some cases. If the witness is a child who has been in some way abused and the culprit is a close relative or family friend it can be very difficult indeed to overcome the child's reluctance to speak. A great deal of sympathy and careful consideration will be required. It may also help to ask a few innocuous questions first to reduce the stress levels of the witness and get him or her accustomed to what is required before you begin dealing with the relevant matters. It is often advisable for the advocates to meet such a witness briefly before the trial so that the faces asking the questions are not wholly unfamiliar.

In England and Wales, rehearsing the witness is not considered appropriate, though ALL witnesses should be asked to read their statements through shortly before they give evidence.

One technique which sometimes works is to ask a hesitant child about an innocent occasion on which he or she was with the defendant and then ask whether the child would go again. The inevitable reply will be '*no*'. If you then ask '*why not*', you will often succeed in persuading the child to tell you the reason.

The reluctant witness is also difficult. This problem should not arise very much if the elementary precaution of having the witness re-read the statement shortly before going into court is adopted. Any reluctance will then emerge at that stage.

If necessary, most witnesses can be compelled to answer (there are some exceptions in relation to spouses – for details consult a book on evidence). But of course even if the witness is told that it is a contempt of court not to answer, it is difficult to obtain the answers you want without asking leading questions. If the witness insists that it is so long ago that he or she can no longer remember, there will in practice be very little you can do. You may need to resort to damage limitation.

The witness who contradicts what is in the witness statement can be dealt with by applying to treat the witness as 'hostile' in a formal sense. If that application is granted it enables the advocate who calls the witness to cross-examine, i.e. to ask leading questions, and even to put the statement to the witness in order to point out the inconsistency. The problem is that to do this effectively destroys the credibility of the witness. If you know a witness is going to do this it is usually better not to call them at all.

Another circumstance worthy of mention is where there is some feature which places significant reservations on the value of the evidence of the witness, for example a witness who has a significant criminal record. In some criminal cases the prosecution rely on the evidence of co-accused who have already pleaded guilty. If you intend to call such a witness it is almost invariably better to deal with the damaging factor yourself in evidence in chief rather than wait for it to emerge in cross-examination. It may even be as well to put reference to it in your opening speech.

Two other matters which often arise in examination-in-chief are the production of exhibits and witnesses who need to refresh their memory from documents. As to the former, if a witness is to produce either a document or a physical object which is to become an exhibit, for example the broken glass which inflicted a wound on the victim of an assault with which the defendant in a criminal trial is charged, all you need to do in examination-in-chief is to produce the evidence that the exhibit was found:

'Q: *Did you find anything significant at the scene?*
A: *Yes, on the floor by the blood stains on the carpet there was the base and part of the sides of a glass.*
Q: *Where is it now?*
A: *In that cardboard box on the table in court.'*

Have the box handed to the witness who will then open it and produce the glass, you should then turn to the judge and say something along the lines of:
'Your honour, may that be exhibit 2 please?'

Finally, many witnesses, particularly police officers, are giving evidence of matters occurring several months before and have dealt with similar incidents in the meantime. Such witnesses often find it difficult to remember details of dates and times, who said what and in what order. If such a witness made a documentary record sufficiently closely following the incident itself that the witness could remember clearly at the time when the document was produced (generally it needs to have been made within about 24 hours) it is possible for the witness to be permitted to refresh his or her memory from the document. The document does not normally become an exhibit and does not go to the jury if there is one, but the witness is permitted to use it in order to give the details of the evidence.

The permission of the court is required so the sequence which needs to be adopted is to ask the witness:

'Q: Would it help you to refer to any document or record you made at or very near the time?
A: Yes, I would like to refer to my pocket notebook.
Q: When was the note made?
A: The incident occurred at about 8 o'clock and I made a note at 10 o'clock when I came off duty.
Q: When you made the note, how good was your memory of what had happened?
A: It was quite clear.'

Then turn to the judge and ask for permission:

'Your honour, may the witness please refer to his pocketbook in order to refresh his memory?

The use by police officers of their notebooks also provides a useful example of when to lead material which may detract from the credibility of the witness rather than leaving it to emerge in cross-examination. Where several police officers have been present at events being described in evidence, it is common practice for them to write their notes together. This enables them to ensure that they do not record inconsistent details, which is important because such inconsistency would leave them vulnerable in cross-examination. However, if the fact that they made the notes together emerges in cross- examination, that of itself can appear suspicious. It is much better to ask in chief:

'Q: When you made the note, were you alone?
A: No. I made the note in conjunction with PC Smith.
Q: Is that normal?
A: Yes it is. We are trained and instructed to do so.'

There is then no risk of the material doing any damage.

3. Cross-Examination

The art of effective cross-examination is without doubt the most difficult of the skills required of an advocate. Some otherwise highly competent advocates never really master it, despite many years in the profession. Even those with a natural flair for it can take years fully to develop their skills.

Nevertheless, it is possible to set out basic guidelines and if you learn them at the outset of your career, bear them in mind while you watch others cross-examine during your pupillage or training contract, and then apply them when you begin practice, they should enable you to carry out a competent cross-examination and will hopefully provide a sound basis for the development of your skills over the years.

There are very few 'rules' as such. Almost every piece of advice which can be given about cross-examination is subject to the reservation that in the particular circumstances of an individual case, it may be necessary to disregard it.

One of the few rules you should never break is that you should invariably prepare very thoroughly. If that message is becoming a little repetitive there is good reason for it!

A detailed knowledge of the area in which the relevant evidence lies is essential. If the cross-examination is of an expert witness, you need at least a basic knowledge of the relevant area of expertise. The technique for cross-examination of an expert will be specifically addressed a little later.

If the witness is dealing with facts, you must know very thoroughly what the background facts are and what all the other available witnesses have said or are expected to say about it. If you realise that a witness is making an assertion which contradicts other evidence you can deal with it, but you will only be able to do so if you know in detail what the other evidence is.

There is, in cross-examination, no prohibition on leading questions and in general you should stick to questions of this type. If you do it will be much easier to keep control of the evidence. You should try as far as possible never to ask a question unless you already know what the answer is or at least you know the answer you expect to get and have contingency plans for what to do if you do not get the expected answer. Cross-examination is not normally an exercise in finding out anything, it is an attempt to alter or devalue the evidence on behalf of the opposition.

Having said that, asking an open question can sometimes pay dividends. In one civil action tried in Chester County Court a few years ago, the claimant's case was that he had sold a taxi firm to the defendant and the full purchase price had not been paid. Counsel for the defendant, having completed a normal and highly competent cross-examination of the claimant, asked why a particular letter in the document bundle was worded in a slightly unusual way. It was an open question and no one other than the witness had any idea what the answer would be. Note, however, that whatever the answer was it was most unlikely that it would do any damage. In fact the claimant said that he had used the wording he had because the business was not actually his to sell. He had given it to a friend a few months earlier! The claim collapsed immediately.

It is, however, very unwise indeed to ask an open question of this type unless you are sure that the answer, whatever it is, can do you no harm.

If the witness has said in evidence in chief anything which is favourable to your case it is usually wise to go over it again to give it extra emphasis and perhaps to obtain some additional material in support of your case. Do so before rather than after you tackle the parts of the evidence you need to challenge and do so by asking leading questions which minimise the risk that the witness will retract or contradict what he or she said in chief.

Two more rules which should never be broken are:

(1) You are required to challenge the witness about each element of his or her evidence which is disputed by your lay client so that the witness has the opportunity to comment on each point. You should normally do so in the structure of your cross-examination as a whole and you should check in planning the cross-examination that you

have done so. To the extent that you have not, you are required to fill in the gaps before you cease cross-examining because, if you have not challenged the witness, it will be assumed that the evidence is not disputed.

(2) You may not put a positive proposition to a witness unless you have a basis for it in the evidence or in your instructions. Leading questions almost invariably involve positive propositions being put to the witness. You may base such a proposition on evidence which has already been heard, on evidence you know is to come, or on instructions you have from your client. Those instructions need not be covered by evidence but you may not make positive assertions of your own. To do so is unethical.

Keeping that in mind, you should plan each cross-examination for each witness. Remember question 5. First, decide in detail what you are trying to achieve. Second, plan in advance how you are going to try to achieve it but do not write a script and be prepared to change tactics if the initial strategy fails.

Do not continue with a strategy which is clearly failing. If you do, you will simply add weight to the evidence you are trying to discredit. If you have a reserve strategy, change to it. If not, do the minimum required to challenge the evidence and then stop.

In all jurisdictions in England and Wales you will almost always have the statements in support of the opposing case well in advance of the trial. If you do not, and if you do not have time to deal with a very late statement, oppose its admission or argue that it should only be admitted if you are given an adjournment to enable you to deal with it, and ask that the opposition should be ordered to pay the costs arising from the adjournment. The only significant exceptions are criminal cases in the Magistrates' Court and when you are prosecuting a criminal case in the Crown Court. Even in such cases you should have a fairly clear idea from the 'advance disclosure' what the witnesses are likely to say.

Take each opposing witness in turn, go through his or her witness statement and decide what evidence the witness is to give which needs to be challenged. Then decide how to challenge it:

As already discussed (in Chapter 3) by far the best way is to call evidence of your own which contradicts the evidence given by the opposing witness. Then all you need to do is to put the evidence to the witness and assert that on the basis of the evidence you have called (or are about to call) the witness under cross-examination must be wrong. You are in any event required to give the witness under cross-examination the opportunity to explain or contradict the evidence you have called or intend to call.

There are, in most cases, three other possible methods. They were set out as items c), d) and e) in part 10 of Chapter 3: in each of the three cases you must include, in one form or another, a question or questions which suggest that the evidence is wrong.

(c) Try to cross-examine the witness into changing his or her mind.

(d) Try, in cross-examination, to throw doubt on the reliability or veracity of the evidence on the basis of factors relating to the evidence itself.

(e) Try, in cross-examination, to throw doubt on the reliability or veracity of the evidence on the basis of factors relating to the witness.

The first of these is often not possible and it is unsafe ever to rely on being able to do it. However, if you can do it, it can be very effective indeed.

The most effective way to do it is to adopt an approach totally devoid of any aggression. You need to appear to the witness to be so reasonable that to disagree with you would be churlish.

As an example, which is based on a real case, take a civil action arising out of a road accident. The claimant for whom you act was a pedestrian who attempted to cross the road and was hit by the defendant's car. Your case is that the car was going too fast, it was a residential street and the driver was not checking for pedestrians as he should have done. His case is that the claimant ran out in front of him and gave him no chance to stop.

A defence witness is called who saw the accident and who asserts that the claimant did emerge into the road at speed. You know from what is in her witness statement that she did not see the claimant until he was off the pavement and already in the road because her view until then was obscured by a delivery van parked partly on the pavement between her and the claimant.

You draw her attention to the relevant part of the witness statement and ask: *'That must mean that he was only in your view for about three or four feet before he was hit, mustn't it?'* She agrees. The way you put the question gave her little choice.

You then add *'So even at a normal walking pace of about four feet per second he was in your view for a second or less, wasn't he?'* Again she can only agree.

You then ask *'So what you really mean is that you saw him _appear_ suddenly from behind the van. You weren't really in a position to judge how fast he was going, were you?'* Again, because of what you have already drawn from the witness it is difficult for her to disagree. She hesitates. You prompt *'To be fair, Mrs Jones, that's right isn't it?'* She responds *'Yes, I suppose it is.'*

Another example occurred in a murder trial at Chester Crown Court in the 1970s. The defence was one of diminished responsibility and the main issue was the mental capacity of the defendant. The prosecution called a psychiatrist who had assessed her IQ at 57, which is very severely below normal. He had nonetheless concluded that she was responsible for her actions. This, as nearly as can be replicated so long afterwards, was the sequence of cross-examination adopted by defence counsel:

'Q: *The average IQ is presumably about a hundred?*

A: *Yes, actually slightly more than that.*

Q: *So in lay terms this defendant has only about half the brains of a normal person?*

A: *I suppose you could put it like that.*

Q: *So if she has only half the brains of a normal person do you really still adhere to the view that she is fully responsible for her actions?'*

A: *Perhaps not.'*

The judge then intervened and directed an acquittal on the charge of murder and the defendant was convicted on her plea of guilty to the lesser offence of manslaughter on the grounds of diminished responsibility.

The second possibility, to attack the reliability of the evidence on grounds inherent within the evidence itself, is much more common and much more readily available. If you can see any weakness in the nature of the evidence, cross-examine with a view to exposing it and emphasising it.

Advocacy and Public Speaking

The factor most commonly relied upon in this type of cross-examination is inconsistency. This may be inconsistency with other evidence in the case or inconsistency with something the same witness has said on another occasion.

As to the former, if you know the case thoroughly you will be able to refer the witness to the evidence already heard or perhaps to evidence you know is to come, and to ask whether in the light of that evidence the witness is sure he or she is correct.

For example, suppose that the witness is the victim of an alleged assault in which he says he was hit three times on the head with a 2 foot iron bar. You are aware that there is only one injury to his head. Cross-examination would proceed something like this:

'Q: Are you sure you were hit hard on the head three times?
A: Certainly I was.
Q: Well as I understand it, there is clear medical evidence from Dr Musgrave that there was only one injury to your head. Can you explain that?
A: Well I was definitely hit three times.
Q: But how can you be hit on the head with an iron bar without it leaving marks?'

How the witness replies will be irrelevant. You have already made the point.

As to the latter, look for inconsistencies between what the witness said in the witness box and what is contained in the witness statement, or statements made by the witness on other occasions. If the witness has made two inconsistent statements in the course of oral evidence this will be particularly telling. Make sure you choose significant inconsistencies. There are few cross-examination tactics which are less effective than a long series of questions about the kind of trivial inconsistencies which arise from the lack of precision in everyday speech.

If you are using a statement made on a previous occasion, try to pick one that is inherently reliable, especially one signed by the witness or at least seen by him or her at the time when it was made.

Be wary of relying on the recital in a medical report, or a report by a hospital triage nurse, of how the patient is said to have described the accident circumstances. Such reports are often inaccurate without any fault on the part of the patient. They are not seen by the patient at the time of writing. Nor are they signed by the patient. If the medical report is later relied upon in support of the claim, the patient does then have the opportunity to say the recital is not correct but very few of them pick up inaccuracies, even serious ones. Some medical consultants dictate what they recall the patient telling them while the patient is still present, on the assumption that if any of the details are wrong the patient will say so, but few ordinary people would have the confidence to interrupt and challenge a consultant physician or surgeon, so the assumption is far from reliable.

Unreliability in evidence is usually the result of mistaken observation by the witness or faulty memory rather than deliberate lying but if you are confronted by a witness who appears to be lying, one useful tactic is to ask for minor peripheral details of the story which are not in the witness statement and are thus unlikely to have been rehearsed. Make a careful mental note of the answers you have been given, go on to something else and then after a few minutes, go back and ask in a different way for the same peripheral details. Unless the witness has a very good memory, you will be given different answers on the second occasion. If the witness claims not to be able to remember the peripheral details, you have a good basis for arguing in your closing speech that this of itself suggests strongly that the story is untrue.

One very clear example is what is known as '**Queen Caroline's Case**'. In 1820 George IV succeeded his father George III. George IV hated his wife Caroline and in order to prevent her becoming Queen, he sought a divorce. At that time, divorce could only be achieved by an Act of Parliament and the only available ground was adultery. A bill alleging adultery was duly presented to Parliament. The allegation was that, while she was Princess of Wales between 1714 and 1717, Caroline had carried on an affair with an Italian servant of the Royal Household, principally in Italy. She adamantly denied the allegation so the evidence was called before the House of Lords commencing on 19 August 1820. A full account of the trial is available online. The main witness was another Italian servant of the Royal Household called Theodore Majocci who spoke no English. When he was cross-examined, counsel for the Queen, Mr Brougham, began asking for peripheral details. The result was that the witness began repeatedly to reply '*Non mi ricordo*' (I do not remember). The report sometimes gives the phrase in English and sometimes in Italian so accurate counting is difficult, but in one form or another he said '*I do not know*' or '*I do not remember*' at least 113 times. The Bill was abandoned before its second reading.

Another obvious example of inherent weakness in evidence is a case based on identification. The dangers of identification evidence are well known. Look for factors which tend to suggest the identification may have been relatively weak. The obvious possibilities are a long distance between the witness and the culprit, poor lighting, an obstruction between the two, only a brief view of the culprit or the lapse of a long time between the original sighting of the culprit and the identification of the defendant. If any of these is present, put to the witness, in the form of a leading question, that the factor was present, for example:

'You were at least 50 yards away when the victim was punched, weren't you?'

'There were eight or 10 other people milling about in the space between you and the victim, weren't there?'

To attack the credibility of the witness is also quite frequent, though far less common than attacking the credibility of the evidence. The obvious example is to cross-examine a witness who has a criminal record involving offences of dishonesty.

You should never attack the character of a witness unless it is a necessary part of your case but if it is necessary you should not hesitate to do it and you should not be deterred by any feelings of sympathy for the witness.

Never resort to arguing with the witness. What you say to the witness should always be a question. If it is based on a positive assertion, which a cross-examination question usually will be, it is simple enough to preface it *'is it not the case that ...'*, or to suffix it *'that's what happened, isn't it?'* Try to avoid the repetitive use of *'I put it to you that...'* which unless used sparingly tends to sound ponderous and pompous. *'I suggest that'*, *'what really happened is ... isn't it?'* and several other expressions can be used equally well. It is best to use a variety of such expressions.

Finally, it may sometimes be necessary to put aggressive questions to a witness or to use staccato phrasing but do so with care. Under no circumstances should you ever shout at or be rude to a witness even if you are accusing them of lying.

It can sometimes be effective to cross-examine very aggressively because this may make the witness angry and an angry witness has far less control of what he or she says, but you should alter the tone, pace and pitch of your voice, not the volume. It is legitimate to set out to appear to be angry but you should never allow yourself to become angry.

There is no need to raise your voice at all and to do so is likely to be counter-productive. A few words spoken very quietly but with the sibilants (S sounds) and plosives (T or D) heavily emphasised and significant pauses between words can sound very aggressive indeed.

4. Cross-Examination of an Expert Witness

The obvious difficulty with cross-examining an expert is that he knows much more about his field of expertise than you do. He or she can very easily respond to a question by using technical language you do not understand. It is worth remembering that the judge also suffers from this disadvantage.

Bear in mind also that the court deciding an issue between experts is carrying out a rather different exercise from that which is required in a non-expert factual dispute. The factor which distinguishes an expert from other witnesses is that the expert is permitted to give evidence of his opinion. The number of cases in which experts lie is so small as to be insignificant. They almost invariably genuinely hold the opinions they advance. In addition the courts accept that without the expertise in the relevant field they cannot judge which expert is technically correct. The decision being taken is which opinion is better argued on the basis that this is more likely to be correct.

'The court has to evaluate the witness and the soundness of his opinion. Most importantly, this involves an examination of the reasons given for his opinions and the extent to which they are supported by the evidence.'
Stuart Smith LJ in **Loveday v Renton** [1990] 1 Med LR 117.

In recent times and in relatively small civil cases, a practice has arisen of appointing a single expert on a joint basis. In many cases this is tantamount to trial by expert because there is very little basis on which to challenge the expert. For obvious reasons such experts are very rarely called. If the expert's evidence is important to the decision, the case usually settles once the expert's report is received.

In cases of any size or weight, there will usually be one expert on each side in each discipline relevant to the case. There is a possibility of arguing that your expert is better qualified but an imbalance sufficient to justify the point is extremely rare. If your expert on flying a glider has 33,000 flying hours and the opposing expert 30,000, there is little point in attempting to rely on the difference. Usually, the only way to cross-examine the other side's expert is to get your own expert to tell you why he or she says the other side's expert is wrong.

There are in broad terms two ways you can do this. The one usually adopted is to have your expert sit next to you in court telling you on a question by question basis what to ask. The problem with this approach is that you will frequently be asking questions and receiving replies which you do not understand. Even at its best the process is time-consuming and tedious.

The alternative, which is very much better if you can do it but which calls, as does everything else in this book, for very thorough preparation, is to buy or borrow a student's book on the field of expertise concerned and acquire a basic knowledge of the subject. Then arrange a conference with your own expert before the trial and get him or her to give you a tutorial on the conflict between the two experts, so that you understand the structure and details of the dispute and why the opposing expert is alleged to be wrong.

The practice of arranging joint reports setting out the points of agreement and disagreement will help with this process but you will need far more detail and a much better knowledge of the background of the subject than will be contained in such a report in order to prepare a cross-examination. The individual conference tutorial prior to the trial is absolutely essential.

You will then be able to ask questions in a much more normal way without the need constantly to refer to your own expert in the courtroom, although you may still need to do so to some extent. The result is likely to be much more effective. You will be able to ask supplemental questions of your own and you will be able to insist that the opposing expert explains his or her hypothesis in a way such that you can understand it. If he or she uses jargon you do not understand ask *'How do you define that term in plain English?'* This method of preparing and presenting a cross-examination will make it very much easier to find and draw attention to any flaws in the hypothesis being advanced by the witness and any respects in which it is not adequately supported by the evidence.

5. Re-Examination

After cross-examination, the advocate who called the witness is permitted to ask further questions. There are however two restrictions:

(a) Once again, leading questions are not permitted.

(b) The matters to which re-examination is directed must have arisen from the cross-examination.

In most cases, re-examination is very brief and only two or three questions are asked in order to clarify answers given in cross-examination. It is not at all unusual for there to be no re-examination at all.

However, if your opponent's cross-examination of your witness has been particularly effective, this is your opportunity to try to repair the damage. It is difficult to suggest in advance how to do this because it depends entirely on the individual circumstances. To repair the damage without asking leading questions is very difficult and may well be impossible. Having said that, questions such as: *'When you said in answer to my learned friend that ... XXXXX ... what did you really mean?'* or: *'You said in examination-in-chief that ... YYYYY ... then in answer to my learned friend you said ... ZZZZZ ... Can you explain?'* may enable the witness to recover some ground.

CHAPTER 7
SPEECHES IN CRIMINAL CASES

The Jury Speech is the reason advocates exist.
Iain Morley QC

The normal order of proceedings in a criminal trial in the Crown Court is as follows:

1. Prosecution opening speech.
2. Prosecution evidence.
3. Defence opening speech (if the defence are to call evidence other than or as well as that of the defendant).
4. Defence evidence.
5. Prosecution closing speech.
6. Defence closing speech.
7. Judge summing up.
8. Jury retirement and verdict.

There are thus potentially four speeches in all and the requirements of all four are different.

The order of speeches in the Magistrates' Court is broadly the same though there are some differences in the details.

In an opening speech for the prosecution in a criminal trial before a jury it is customary to begin by introducing both yourself and your opponent. For example:

'Members of the Jury, my name is Hartley Shawcross and I appear for the Prosecution. The defendant, Oliver Spiral, who is 37 years of age, is represented by my learned friend Mr F E Smith.'

You should then set out the facts in chronological order. HH Judge Robin David, QC, for many years the Resident Judge at Chester Crown Court, often used to say: *'When opening a criminal case to a jury, tell them the story.'*
Where the facts are disputed you should make this clear and you should set out the evidence upon which you intend to rely.

Follow this by listing the charges in the indictment, explaining the legal structure of each, why you say the defendant is guilty and how you propose to prove it.

Finally tell them that the prosecution bear the burden of proof in a criminal case and that the standard of proof is that they must be sure of guilt before they can convict. It is suggested that you conclude with words such as: *'The prosecution has to prove the case so that you are sure of guilt on each charge before you can convict on that Count. When you have heard the evidence in this case it is my submission that you will have not the slightest doubt as to the guilt of this defendant on each of these charges and that you should convict the defendant accordingly.'*

In the other three speeches, introduction of the personalities involved in the case is not necessary. If you are to make an opening speech for the defence, explain the defendant's case in chronological order, list the evidence you intend to call and tell the jury why it is relevant and what you are seeking to establish.

The closing speech should have been composed, at least in outline, when you first began to prepare the case. Remember **Q2** in Chapter 3: *'How can I address the tribunal in order to convince them and what material do I need in order to be able to make that address?'*

You should now fill out the structure in the light of the evidence as it has emerged and modify it as necessary in relation to any evidence you have not been able to obtain. Review the evidence on both sides, draw attention to any strengths in your own case or weaknesses in the opposition's case by reminding the jury of what was said by the witnesses or what is written in the documents. If you are prosecuting, keep the speech unemotional and matter-of-fact. If you are defending, it is entirely appropriate to resort to every rhetorical skill you can muster and to make an emotional speech if you think this will give your client the maximum chance of the best outcome.

In cases where the defendant pleads guilty, there will usually be two relatively short speeches, one for the prosecution outlining the facts of the case, one for the defence which is almost always aimed at minimising the sentence and is called a 'Plea In Mitigation'. Both will be relatively brief. Where there is a single defendant, such a case usually lasts only about half an hour in total.

The objective of the prosecution opening is to give the court the facts it needs to decide the appropriate sentence. Accordingly, the prosecution advocate will usually:

(a) Introduce himself or herself and the advocate(s) for the defendant(s).
(b) State the name and age of the (or each) defendant.
(c) Give a brief outline of the facts of the offence, or if there are several charges, of each of them. If there are several offences it is almost invariably best to keep them in chronological order.
(d) If appropriate, give brief details of the impact on the victim.
(e) Say how, where and when the defendant (or each defendant) was apprehended and his or her response when questioned and charged.
(f) Summarise any previous criminal record of the (or each) defendant.
(g) Inform the court of any offences which have not to be charged but which the defendant wishes to have taken into consideration when sentence is passed.

It is important to remember that what is required in items (c), (d) and (e) is a simple summary of the facts. No detailed analysis of the evidence is required as it would be in opening a case for a trial. For example:

'This was a burglary of a house in Ellesmere Port owned by Mr and Mrs Sutton. It was committed in daylight on (date) while the owners were away on holiday. Entry was gained by forcing a rear patio door, apparently with a crowbar. An

untidy search was made but no other damage was done. Jewellery valued at £2,500 and about £300 in cash was taken. Some of the jewellery was of very high sentimental value to Mrs Sutton. None of it was ever recovered. The Defendant's fingerprints were found at the scene and he was arrested three days later at his home in Chester. He was interviewed and admitted the offence saying that he had already sold the stolen jewellery in a local public house the day after the offence in order to obtain money for drugs.'

If you are to make a plea in mitigation, the object to be achieved is to keep the sentence to a minimum, so the task is to identify, assemble and present the material available which will have this effect.

By far the most significant factor in deciding sentence is the nature and seriousness of the offence(s). After that the most common mitigation factors are:

(a) A confession and a guilty plea, and the earlier the better.

(b) Any clear expression of remorse.

(c) Any attempt to mitigate the consequences of the offence, such as help given to the police to recover the stolen property.

(d) The absence or relative lack of seriousness of any previous criminal record, or the lack of any record for similar offences.

(e) Anything particularly creditable in the offender's past, for example, distinction in military service or an act of bravery.

Speeches in Criminal Cases

You should see the lay client before the hearing (often this will be done by a barrister on the morning of the hearing), go through the facts of the case and his or her history so that you can identify the mitigating factors available. The speech will simply be giving the court the list of relevant items and asking for the minimum sentence for the client.

After you have been in practice for a few years, it can become difficult to think of anything new to say in a plea in mitigation. One advocate in Chester used often to use an analogy that his client *'Stood at the crossroads'* of his life where the court had a choice as to whether he could be put on probation (again) or whether only immediate imprisonment would suffice. One morning at the Crown Court in Dolgellau, when the advocate concerned had several cases in the list, HH Judge David Morgan-Hughes observed *'It is becoming rather crowded at that crossroads Mr *****'*.

CHAPTER 8

ETHICS AND PROFESSIONAL CONDUCT

Face the complexity involved in making ethical choices.
Linda Fisher Thornton

1. Introduction

A full analysis of the professional conduct rules involved in practice at the bar or as a solicitor is beyond the scope of this book. This chapter is concerned with the ethical/ professional conduct requirements of each profession only in so far as they affect the conduct of an advocate in, and as ancillary to, the preparation and presentation of a case in court.

The behaviour of an advocate in relation to his or her lay client is largely governed by two distinct and wholly separate regimes, the professional conduct rules and the law relating to legal professional privilege. In many areas of practice the two overlap to a considerable extent but it is essential to understand that the two are not the same, they have no direct link and they often have very different effects.

The Code of Conduct for members of the bar ('BCOC') is published by the Bar Standards Board on behalf of the Bar Council and can be downloaded as a PDF file, free of charge, from the Bar Council website. At the time of writing the latest edition was the 1st edition published in January 2014. The corresponding code for solicitors was until 6 October 2011 published by the

Law Society as 'The Solicitors' Code of Conduct' ('SCOC') but on that date was replaced by a new code published by the Solicitors Regulation Authority ('SRACOC'). The SRA Handbook which contains this Code is available in HTML or as a PDF file, free of charge, from the SRA website. At the time of writing, the current edition is Version 12 published on 31 October 2014. The BSB Handbook and the SRA Handbook are each substantially larger than this book.

The relevant section of BCOC is called 'The Core Duties'. These duties are set out as follows:

'CD1:   *You must observe your duty to the court in the administration of justice.*

CD2:   *You must act in the best interests of each client.*

CD3:   *You must act with honesty and integrity.*

CD4:   *You must maintain your independence.*

CD5:   *You must not behave in a way which is likely to diminish the trust and confidence which the public places in you or in the profession.*

CD6:   *You must keep the affairs of each client confidential.*

CD7:   *You must provide a competent standard of work and service to each client.*

CD8:   *You must not discriminate unlawfully against any person.*

CD9: *You must be open and co-operative with your regulators.*

CD10: *You must take reasonable steps to manage your practice, or carry out your role within your practice, competently and in such a way as to achieve compliance with your legal and regulatory obligations.'*

The corresponding section of the SCOC was called 'The Principles'. These principles were set out as follows:

'You must:

1. *Uphold the rule of law and the proper administration of justice.*

2. *Act with integrity.*

3. *Not allow your independence to be compromised.*

4. *Act in the best interests of each client.*

5. *Provide a proper standard of service to your clients.*

6. *Behave in a way that maintains the trust the public places in you and in the provision of legal services.*

7. *Comply with your legal and regulatory obligations and deal with your regulators and ombudsmen in an open timely and co-operative manner.*

8.   *Run your business or carry out your role in the business effectively and in accordance with proper governance and sound financial and risk management principles.*

9.   *Run your business or carry out your role in the business in a way that encourages equality of opportunity and respect for diversity.*

10. *Protect client money and assets.'*

As is readily apparent, there was very little difference between the professional conduct rules of the two professions. However, the newly introduced SRACOC is drafted on an entirely different basis. It refers to this as *'an outcomes based approach'*. The outcomes to be achieved are listed as follows:

'You must achieve these outcomes:

O (1.1)   *you treat your clients fairly;*

O (1.2)   *you provide services to your clients in a manner which protects their interests in their matter, subject to the proper administration of justice;*

O (1.3)   *when deciding whether to act, or terminate your instructions, you comply with the law and the Code;*

O (1.4)   *you have the resources, skills and procedures to carry out your clients' instructions;*

O (1.5)   *the service you provide to clients is competent, delivered in a timely manner and takes account of your clients' needs and circumstances;*

O (1.6)   *you only enter into fee agreements with your clients that are legal, and which you consider are suitable for the client's needs and take account of the client's best interests;*

O (1.7)   *you inform clients whether and how the services you provide are regulated and how this affects the protections available to the client;*

O (1.8)   *clients have the benefit of your compulsory professional indemnity insurance and you do not exclude or attempt to exclude liability below the minimum level of cover required by the SRA Indemnity Insurance Rules;*

O (1.9)   *clients are informed in writing at the outset of their matter of their right to complain and how complaints can be made;*

O (1.10)   *clients are informed in writing, both at the time of engagement and at the conclusion of your complaints procedure, of their right to complain to the Legal Ombudsman, the time frame for doing so and full details of how to contact the Legal Ombudsman;*

O (1.11)   *clients' complaints are dealt with promptly, fairly, openly and effectively;*

O (1.12) *clients are in a position to make informed decisions about the services they need, how their matter will be handled and the options available to them;*

O (1.13) *clients receive the best possible information, both at the time of engagement and when appropriate as their matter progresses, about the likely overall cost of their matter;*

O (1.14) *clients are informed of their right to challenge or complain about your bill and the circumstances in which they may be liable to pay interest on an unpaid bill;*

O (1.15) *you properly account to clients for any financial benefit you receive as a result of your instructions;*

O (1.16) *you inform current clients if you discover any act or omission which could give rise to a claim by them against you.'*

Of these, no less than six (1.9, 1.10, 1.11, 1.12, 1.14, 1.16) are concerned with client's complaints, two (1.6, 1.13) with fees and costs and two (1.7, 1.8) with regulation and insurance. Only 1.1 to 1.5 have any relevance to the conduct of a case in court and they say, in much less detail and with far less precision, much the same as the old rules did.

Because the three codes of conduct are so similar in the relevant areas, in the following parts of this chapter, references to what you must do or not do are made without distinguishing between the two professions except in the few instances where there are significant differences.

2. Obey the Law

Like every other citizen, you must first obey both the civil and criminal law. Parliament is supreme in the UK, and it can and does from time to time override the professional conduct rules and what would otherwise be privilege. If an Act of Parliament requires you to do something you must do it even if it would otherwise be a breach of the rules of professional conduct or a breach of privilege.

The main areas where this is likely to arise involve disclosure of what would otherwise be confidential information. It is not possible to provide an exhaustive list but the most common examples are:

(a) There are a number of provisions about money laundering in the Proceeds of Crime Act 2002.

(b) There are requirements to give information in relation to insolvent companies in the Insolvency Act 1986.

(c) There are duties of disclosure in the Terrorism Act 2000.

The SCOC also used to provide that the duty of confidentiality was overridden where a solicitor was in possession of information derived from the lay client which, if disclosed to the authorities, would enable them to prevent the commission of a criminal offence which was likely to cause significant physical harm to somebody. The duty was also overridden where the disclosure could prevent serious harm to children. The 2007 version of the SCOC contained (in its guidance notes) the following:

'12. *You may reveal confidential information to the extent that you believe necessary to prevent the client or a third party committing a criminal act that you reasonably believe is likely to result in serious bodily harm.*

13. *There may be exceptional circumstances involving children where you should consider revealing confidential information to an appropriate authority. This may be where the child is the client and the child reveals information which indicates continuing sexual or other physical abuse but refuses to allow disclosure of such information. Similarly, there may be situations where an adult discloses abuse either by himself or herself or by another adult against a child but refuses to allow any disclosure. You must consider whether the threat to the child's life or health, both mental and physical, is sufficiently serious to justify a breach of the duty of confidentiality.'*

This wording is not reproduced in the 2011 code. The only equivalent is:

'If you are a litigator or an advocate there may be occasions when your obligation to act in the best interests of a client may conflict with your duty to the court. In such situations you may need to consider whether the public interest is best served by the proper administration of justice and should take precedence over the interests of your client.'

The BCOC does not and never did contain any similar form of words. Suffice it to say that it cannot be the case that any member of either profession could be expected to remain silent when he or she knew that by disclosure they could prevent the commission of a serious criminal offence or serious abuse of a child.

We do advise very firmly indeed that if you ever encounter a problem of this nature you take advice from senior members of your profession, your professional regulatory body or possibly even independent legal advice before you decide what to do.

3. The Duty to the Court

This duty overrides every other duty except the duty to comply with the law and it is difficult to envisage any circumstance in which the duty to obey the law could ever come into conflict with the duty owed to the court.

Subject to that reservation, the overriding duty to which any advocate is subject is to the court and to the administration of justice. In practical terms this means that you must never mislead a court either deliberately or recklessly. Moreover, if you discover that you have inadvertently misled the court by making a statement that you believed was true at the time when you made it but later discover is not, you must correct the matter at the earliest possible opportunity.

A caveat is required as to the word 'know' in this context. You 'know' something if and only if:

(i) You are aware of it from your own knowledge or perception, or

(ii) It is part of your instructions from your client.

In many cases, particularly in criminal defence work, you may be acting for a client against whom there is a very strong, possibly even an overwhelming case. You may, in your own mind, be of the view that he or she is very probably guilty. That does not mean that you 'know' they are guilty. If you have reached such a conclusion, and it is best to avoid doing so, keep it strictly to yourself and do not allow it to affect your conduct of the case in any way. The decision as to the guilt of the defendant is not yours to take. However strong the case against a person is, that person has a right to have his or her own case put by an independent advocate to the limit of the advocate's ability consistent with the rules.

If you have reached the conclusion, on reading the papers, that the client is very likely to be convicted, which is not the same as deciding that he or she is guilty, you should have advised him or her of this at an early stage and you should have discussed the options for changing the strategy (see Chapter 3). If, despite this, the client insists that he or she is innocent, you must do the very best you can, consistent with the rules, to present the case.

From now on, in this chapter, unless otherwise indicated, the word 'know' is used to mean you have seen or heard it yourself or it is in your instructions.

There are a number of practical aspects to this overriding duty to the court and to justice:

(1) Never call a witness if you know the evidence to be given is not true unless you have told the court in advance that that is what you are going to do.

(2) Never produce evidence in any other form which contains anything you know to be false unless you have told the court in advance that that is what you are going to do.

(3) Never make submissions, representations or any other statements which contain anything you know to be false or misleading.

(4) Never put a question to a witness in a form which involves a positive statement if that statement is in any way untrue or misleading.

(5) If you are advancing a legal argument, and in the course of your research you encounter either a decided case or a statutory provision which is contrary to your argument, you must provide the case or statute to the court.

It is rare for an advocate to 'know' any of the facts of the case other than on instructions. If he or she does have significant personal knowledge it will usually be impossible for him or her to take the case at all because of the risk of conflict between the duty to the court and the duty to the client.

Usually, there is no duty to volunteer information to the court and your duty to keep your client's affairs confidential would prevent you from making any such disclosure. However, if you can see that the court will, through lack of information, act unlawfully, you are under a duty to prevent it. This is a rare event but not unknown. The most likely circumstance is if you know that your lay client has previous convictions which dictate that the court must pass a minimum sentence and the prosecution do not inform the court. If that happens and your client will not allow you to disclose the information to the court, you will be faced with an irreconcilable conflict and you must cease to act in the case. Having ceased to act, you must not reveal the information.

A very rare occurrence, which can be extraordinarily difficult to deal with, is a client in a criminal defence case who tells you that he is guilty of the offence but nevertheless wishes to have you conduct a trial on his behalf. Theoretically this can be done but you must be scrupulously careful not to mislead the court. You may test the evidence by open questions, you may even ask each witness questions such as *are you sure that is correct* but you must not put any closed question which contains any assertion inconsistent with guilt. You may submit to the court and the jury that the case is not proved but you may not submit that your client is innocent.

4. Duties to the Lay Client

In essence there are five duties to the lay client, and they override anything else except the duty to the Court and the duty to obey the law. They are:

1) Competence
2) Confidentiality
3) Effort
4) Integrity
5) Independence.

As an advocate, whether a barrister or solicitor, you owe a duty to your client to possess and use skills reasonably competent to the task undertaken. This is no more than a restatement by those responsible for professional conduct of the general duty owed in contract by any person employed in a professional capacity:

'*When a skilled labourer, artisan or artist is employed, there is on his part an implied warranty that he is of skill reasonably competent to the task he undertakes – Spondes peritiam artis* [he undertakes skill in his art]. *Thus, if an apothecary, a watchmaker or an attorney be employed for reward they each impliedly undertake to possess and exercise reasonable skill in their several arts ... An express promise or express representation in the particular case is not necessary.*'
(Willes J in **Harmer v Cornelius** (1858) 141 ER 94)

So, you must be competent. Among many other aspects, this means that you should never accept the conduct of a case which requires skills or knowledge that you do not have unless you are sure you can obtain it in the course of preparing the case.

Subject to the rules and the law, you are required to do everything you possibly can to advance your client's case and interests to the limit of your ability. You must do so without any regard to the consequences to yourself or anybody else.

You must keep your client's affairs confidential, save to the extent necessary to comply with the law and in accordance with the client's instructions. The duty of confidentiality is extreme. Even if a major crime has been committed and remains undetected and your client tells you that he committed it, you must not impart that information to anybody without your client's consent. You cannot normally be forced to answer any question about the instructions given to you by your client because communications between you and the client are privileged and the privilege is the client's, not yours.

The only exception is the one referred to at the end of section 1 of this chapter where the client gives you information that a significant criminal offence, or abuse of a child, is going to be committed in the future which you can prevent by disclosure.

If you are ever put in a position where your duty to the court or the law conflicts with your duty to the client and you need time to take instructions, inform the court immediately that you are *'in danger of being professionally embarrassed'*. (If it is a jury case, ask the court to convene without the jury.) That phrase will tell the court that you have such a conflict without revealing anything confidential and a judge faced with that phrase will understand the general nature of the problem and will be likely to give you as much time as you reasonably need to resolve it.

In addition to the duty not to disclose information given to you by the client or information obtained about him or her as a result of your instructions, there is also a duty to disclose to the client any information in your possession which is of relevance to the case. This duty applies to members of both professions. The exceptions are:

(a)   Where you have expressly told your client that you have information you are either not able or not willing to disclose and he has agreed to instruct you to continue on that basis.

(b)   Where you are prohibited by law from making the disclosure, for example where you have information covered by the Official Secrets Act.

(c)   Where you have been ordered by the court not to make the disclosure. This is very rare in criminal cases but it does happen occasionally at the pre-trial stage in civil and family cases.

(d) The SRACOC also provides that information need not be given to the lay client if the result would be that any person would suffer significant harm. The BCOC contains no parallel provision but in the authors' opinion it is nonetheless to be implied. Certainly you must not provide information to your client which would cause or enable him or her to commit a criminal offence because to do so could make you guilty of the crime, in that you 'aided, abetted, counselled or procured' its commission, and you must not break the criminal law.

This duty of disclosure to a client rarely causes complications for barristers but it can cause difficulties for solicitors where the same solicitors' firm acts for two clients and one client provides the solicitor with information which would be of use to the other client in a different case. The result is that information comes from one client to a solicitor which is protected by the duty of confidentiality to the first client but the information would be useful to the second client in a different case, thus making it subject to the duty to disclose it to the second client. The usual method of dealing with it is either to erect some sort of information barrier within the firm or by ceasing to act for one client or often both.

Every advocate also owes duties to the client to act with independence and integrity, but they are general requirements anyway.

5. Public Duties

A barrister or solicitor is expected to behave with honesty and integrity at all times and not to do anything calculated to reduce the public confidence in the profession. The commission of any criminal offence other than very minor matters such as speeding or illegal parking would lead to you being disbarred or struck off.

You are also required not to abuse your position as an advocate. Accordingly:

(1) You must not put a positive proposition to a witness unless your instructions or the available evidence or other material supports it.

(2) You should not attack the character of a witness or ask questions of a witness which are humiliating, insulting or annoying unless it is necessary to your client's case.

(3) You should not conduct a defence in a criminal case which involves a positive assertion that someone other than your client committed the offence unless it is essential to your client's case.

(4) You should not call any evidence involving a serious allegation against a witness in the case without giving the witness in cross-examination the opportunity to answer the allegation.

(5) You should not suggest to a witness that he is the guilty party unless it is essential to your client's case and you have instructions or other material on which to base the allegation.

(6) If you assert that someone other than a witness is the guilty party, you should avoid naming that party unless it is necessary to your client's case.

(7) You must not put forward to the court any personal expression of opinion as to the facts or the law unless the court invites you to do so. You may say *'It is my submission that ...'* or *'It is my client's case that ...'* or *'I suggest that ...'*. You may not say *'I believe that ...'* or *'I think that...'*.

(8) The same duties apply to allegations made in pleadings (statements of case) or other court documents as apply in relation to questions or assertions in court.

(9) You must not make an allegation of fraud unless you have clear instructions to do so and reasonably credible material which gives rise to an arguable case.

(10) You must not draft a witness statement which contains anything that you do not expect the witness to say.

(11) You must not encourage a witness to give evidence which is untruthful or misleading.

(12) You must not communicate with a witness about the case during the course of his or her evidence without the permission of the court or the consent of the opposing advocate.

(13) There is a specific provision in the BCOC which prohibits coaching a witness. There is no similar provision in the SRACOC, but the practice is nonetheless frowned upon in this country.

(14) You must not put yourself in a position where your own interests conflict with those of your client. If this arises without your being able to prevent it, you should advise the client and either act against your own interests or cease to act.

6. Administrative Duties

As an advocate of either description you are required to cooperate with your disciplinary body and to run your practice/business in a proper manner, consistent with the principles of health and safety, honesty and integrity and lack of unlawful discrimination.

CHAPTER 9

ALTERNATIVE DISPUTE RESOLUTION

Many cases occur in which it is perfectly clear that, by means of a reference to Arbitration, the real interests of the parties will be much better satisfied than they could be by any litigation in a Court of Justice.

The Earl of Mexborough v Bower (1843) 49 ER 1101, 7 Beav. 132. **Lord Langdale MR**

1. What is ADR?

If you become a practising lawyer, it will be vital to consider all of the options available to your client – going to court is not the only method of resolving the issue, and is quite often not the best, cheapest or quickest way to achieve what your client wants. In fact, great emphasis is placed on court being a last resort, so it is important for any lawyer to be aware of other methods. These methods are referred to as Alternative Dispute Resolution, which is usually shortened to ADR. The shorter form is used throughout the rest of this chapter.

Strictly, ADR refers to any means of settling a case or dispute other than by trial in a court. Using this definition, by far the most common form of ADR is **Negotiation** between the parties, either themselves or through their lawyers. Over 80% of civil actions pending or commenced in England and Wales are settled before trial, mostly by this method. In large civil claims it is common for the parties to arrange a **Joint Settlement Meeting** at which all parties and their legal teams are present so that they can try to negotiate a settlement. Many family cases and even quite a large number of criminal trials are also settled or shortened by negotiation.

Direct negotiation is attempted by lawyers in virtually every case as a matter of course. However, the term ADR is most often used to refer to a method of achieving settlement which involves the intervention of a third party.

Using that definition, the most common forms of ADR are **Arbitration**, **Mediation**, **Neutral Evaluation** and **Ombudsman Schemes**.

2. Types of ADR

In **Arbitration** the dispute is resolved by the decision of an independent third party rather than by a judge sitting in a court. It is often used where the dispute involves complex issues which require specialist knowledge and the arbitrator chosen will be an expert with the requisite knowledge.

Arbitration is very frequently encountered in disputes arising from major or complex contracts. Such contracts commonly contain 'arbitration clauses' in which the parties agree in advance that any dispute arising from the contract will be referred to arbitration. The clause usually provides for how the arbitrator is to be identified and appointed and for the scope and form of the arbitration.

Arbitration clauses (which must be in writing, although 'in writing' has an extended definition) are very frequently found in building contracts because the resolution of a building dispute usually requires the specialist knowledge of an expert such as an architect, a structural engineer or a quantity surveyor, so arbitration by such an expert is obviously sensible. Virtually all the standard form contracts published by the professional bodies for use in building contracts contain such clauses.

Where there is no arbitration clause, even when the dispute does not arise from a contract, it is always open to the parties to agree after the dispute has arisen that it should be decided by an arbitrator, though agreements made after the dispute has arisen are relatively rare.

Arbitrations, like court cases, vary enormously. At one end of the scale they can involve huge multinational contracts and many millions of pounds can be at stake. As you might expect, such arbitrations will be conducted on all sides by highly trained and highly specialised lawyers and other professionals. At the other end of the scale an arbitration hearing may arise from a dispute in a minor building contract in which the amount at stake is in thousands rather than millions and in which the arbitrator is a surveyor and the cases on both sides are conducted by local solicitors, counsel who are not specialists, or even by the parties themselves.

All arbitrations where the 'seat of the arbitration' is in England and Wales are governed by the Arbitration Act 1996. The Act contains some provisions which are mandatory and apply irrespective of the agreement of the parties, and other provisions which are not mandatory and can be varied or excluded by agreement. The policy of the Act is to allow the parties as much freedom as possible. Section 1(b) provides:

'the parties should be free to agree how their disputes are resolved, subject only to such safeguards as are necessary in the public interest.'

The result of this is that the parties can agree almost any form of process including an arbitration by written submissions, but in most cases they specify an oral hearing and if so, the arbitration hearing is usually very similar to a court case. Each side presents its case, calling witnesses (who are examined and cross-examined, etc.), producing documents and making opening and closing submissions, including any legal arguments. The arbitrator then gives his or her decision, usually subsequently in writing. The Arbitrator will usually have power to award costs in much the same way as does a judge, though this is not among the mandatory provisions (sections 59 and 61).

The mandatory provisions of the Act include powers to act in support of an arbitrator, for example to summon witnesses, and residual powers for the court to control the arbitration if necessary, though the courts are very reluctant to intervene and will not usually do so unless the conduct of the arbitrator is wholly unreasonable or leads to a substantial injustice.

The mandatory provisions make the arbitrator's decision binding on the parties in that it can be enforced by the courts. They also provide a right of appeal to the court from the decision of an arbitrator if it is based on an error of law.

If a party to a contract containing an arbitration clause ignores it and begins a court claim based on a dispute, the other party has a choice. The defendant can rely on the clause and apply to the court under section 9 of the

Act to postpone the action, which the court is normally required to do under section 9(4). Alternatively, the defendant can defend the action in the usual way. An application under section 9 has to be made after acknowledging receipt of the proceedings but before taking any substantive step to defend the action (section 9(3)) so the decision to defend the action in the normal way is usually irreversible.

Mediation is wholly different. A mediator seeks to negotiate an agreement between the parties to settle the case and he or she succeeds only if such an agreement is reached. If not, mediation is said to have failed and the court case continues to a trial if necessary. What happened at an unsuccessful attempt at mediation cannot be used as evidence at any subsequent trial though it may, if it is relevant, be used after the trial in relation to costs.

The role of a mediator is essentially one of shuttle diplomacy. He or she will begin with each party separately and establish, in relation to each, what they want from the case, what they are willing to concede and as far as possible what is the minimum they are willing to accept. He or she will then compare the two positions and see whether they can be reconciled. If they are clearly too far apart, the attempt may be abandoned at this stage. If they are close enough together to make agreement seem feasible the mediator will try to coax each towards the position of the other until there is sufficient common ground to make an agreement possible. The mediator will then usually bring the parties face to face and negotiate the fairest possible agreement to resolve the dispute.

Like an arbitrator, a mediator will often be an expert in the field relevant to the dispute but mediation in itself is a highly specialised task and training is essential. The skill is to achieve enough movement from each side to enable an agreement to be reached but yet to be fair between the parties and especially not to push one side harder than the other.

Mediation is the form of third party ADR most frequently resorted to by the courts or with the encouragement of the courts in pending or threatened litigation. It is successful in the vast majority of cases in which it is attempted. A pioneering Mediation Scheme was set up in The Civil Justice Centre at Chester in 2005. It ran for over two years and it managed to settle just over 80% of the cases referred to it. Unfortunately, it was then replaced by a national scheme which was subsequently abandoned due to low usage, though many courts now have salaried mediators working particularly in Small Claims cases and their success rate is generally over 70%.

Parties who are legally represented will usually have their lawyers participate in the mediation.

Neutral Evaluation is not common in the UK but is popular in some other jurisdictions, including the USA. The evaluator is presented with the cases for both parties, either at a hearing or in writing and he or she considers them and expresses a view as to the relative strengths and weaknesses of each. This view is not binding on the parties but they will take it into account in subsequent negotiations because if the Evaluator arrives at the conclusion that at trial A or B would be likely to win, that view is probably correct. As a result, the process often leads to a negotiated settlement which would not otherwise have occurred. Lawyers may or may not be involved on behalf of the parties.

An **Ombudsman** is an independent person appointed to deal with complaints by members of the public about various public bodies or those in the private sector providing services to the public in a particular area. Most have been set up by the government and have their authority from legislation. Some have been set up by agreement between those providing the services.

Ombudsmen provide facilities for those in dispute with public bodies or organisations providing services to obtain rulings on the disputes and usually recommendations as to an appropriate remedy without recourse to the courts.

There are many ombudsman schemes in the UK. They differ widely in the details of how to complain, what powers they have, whether their decisions are enforceable or advisory, and particularly the time limits applicable to making a complaint. However, they almost all have the following in common:

Alternative Dispute Resolution

(a) Their services are free.

(b) There is usually no bill for costs payable by a person whose complaint is not upheld and no provision for recovery of legal costs by the person making the complaint.

(c) Complaints are dealt with in writing.

(d) An Ombudsman will usually not act unless the applicant has exhausted his rights of complaint within the organisation or body subject to the complaint.

(e) They will not usually act if litigation on the subject matter has been commenced.

(f) Their recommendations, even if not strictly enforceable, will usually be honoured by the body or organisation against which a complaint is upheld.

(g) There is no appeal from the decision.

(h) The time limits are generally very much shorter than those for litigation (typically six or 12 months as opposed to three or six years for most litigation).

The combination of these factors usually means that those making complaints do not use lawyers. Nevertheless you need to know about such schemes because you may well need to advise a client that he or she would be better advised to make a complaint to the relevant Ombudsman than to commence risky litigation.

A decision by an Ombudsman does not usually debar subsequent litigation by a party seeking to obtain a different result from the court, but because of the risk in costs if the court comes to the same decision as the Ombudsman, such claims are rare.

Ombudsmen in the UK and Ireland have a professional body, The Ombudsman Association. Membership is not compulsory but almost all ombudsmen are members. The Association's website:

www.ombudsmanassociation.org

is a very useful source of information about the various schemes available.

3. The Benefits and Detriments of ADR

In most cases, ADR, in whatever form, is quicker, cheaper and more efficient than litigation, which always has an element of risk and usually very serious costs consequences for whoever loses. The benefits and detriments of the various forms of ADR are, however, different.

If a dispute involves complex decisions based on specialist knowledge it is very cumbersome for a court to deal with it. In a case of any size each party will rely on an expert witness in each area of knowledge. The experts will usually disagree about the key factors and the judge, who will usually have no expertise at all in the relevant field, is called upon to decide which expert is more probably correct. As was pointed out in Chapter 6, part 4 (cross-examination of an expert), the courts acknowledge that they cannot decide who is correct. The only decision possible is who can best justify his argument by reference to the evidence.

In the majority of cases the expert who can best justify his argument from the evidence is likely to be the one who is right, but this is far from certain. He or she may simply be much more articulate than the opposing expert, or the scientific research which would establish with certainty who is correct may not yet have been done.

It is obviously more efficient for such a case to be submitted to arbitration by an expert in the relevant field of knowledge. Such a tribunal is much more likely to be able to tell who is correct. He or she will also be able to understand the technical argument immediately. The evidence in support of competing arguments will thus be dealt with very much more quickly than it would before a judge without the specialist knowledge, although the Courts of Justice can and do provide judges with specialist knowledge in some fields.

The main detriment is that the Arbitrator will often not be a trained lawyer (although he or she will almost certainly have had training in arbitration which will have included some analysis of the law and the procedural rules). The result is that he or she may make an error of law or procedure which results in an appeal. On appeal there is likely to be an oral hearing at which the award may well be set aside. If this happens, it will add very substantially to the costs.

In addition, arbitrators do not have the same powers as courts to dispose in a summary manner of cases or parts of cases which are certain or virtually certain to fail, or to give summary judgement in cases or parts of cases which are certain or virtually certain to succeed. Cases where such an order would have been made by a court can actually take considerably longer if they are subjected to arbitration.

The benefits of mediation are very wide and compelling:

Alternative Dispute Resolution

(a) If the court has a salaried mediator, his services to the parties in the dispute are free. Even if a mediator has to be brought in by the parties and paid, the expense will usually be relatively modest compared with the cost of litigation.

(b) The mediator proceeds by persuading the parties to agree so the case only settles if each party (one of whom may be your client) is prepared to consent to the result. Hence, both parties usually go home satisfied with the result, which is very seldom the case after contested litigation.

(c) The agreement can include terms which are outside the powers of a court. For example, take a dispute where a claimant asserts that he has a private right of way across the defendant's land. The existence of the right of way along the alleged route would be very inconvenient for the defendant, who denies that there is a right of way. The court can only say whether the right does or does not exist along the alleged route, but a mediator could negotiate a settlement for the creation of a right of way with a different route which is equally convenient to the claimant but much less inconvenient to the defendant.

(d) If mediation succeeds this is invariably very much quicker and cheaper than contested litigation.

The only real disadvantage is that if mediation fails, it will have added to the costs of the litigation, which will then have to be resumed.

Much the same applies to Neutral Evaluation. If it does lead to a settlement it is quicker, cheaper and each party ends up with something to which he or she was prepared to consent. If the Evaluation does not lead to a settlement, it adds to the costs.

There are very few disadvantages to the use of an Ombudsman. Because the service is free, is subject specific and has no costs penalty if the complaint is not upheld, it is very often much better for the client to use an ombudsman if the subject of the dispute is within the remit of one of the schemes. The only real drawbacks are that disputes are very often not covered by one of the schemes or sometimes that the remedies available under the scheme are not adequate.

4. Why use ADR?

Because ADR is very often quicker, cheaper and more efficient than litigation, as a professional advocate with a duty to give the best possible advice to your clients, you may well need to tell clients that they would be better advised to agree to arbitration, to try mediation or to make the complaint to a relevant ombudsman, than to embark upon or continue with litigation.

In addition, ADR, and particularly mediation, is increasingly used at the behest of the courts in litigation which is pending or has already begun. The rules place a specific duty on the court to encourage and facilitate ADR if appropriate. There are guidelines on this in the Civil Procedure Rules (CPR) and the Family Procedure Rules (FPR).

The court has a duty to further the overriding objective by actively managing cases. This requirement is contained in Rule 1.4 of both the CPR and the FPR, and in Rule 1.4(2) for both sets of rules, this includes:

'encouraging the parties to use an alternative dispute resolution procedure if the court considers that appropriate and facilitating the use of such procedure'

and

'helping the parties to settle the whole or part of the case'.

In civil proceedings, section II of the Practice Direction on Pre-Action Conduct published in April 2010 ('The Approach of The Courts') provides:

'4.1 The CPR enable the court to take into account the extent of the parties' compliance with this Practice Direction or a relevant pre-action protocol (see paragraph 5.2) when giving directions for the management of claims (see CPR rules 3.1(4) and (5) and 3.9(1) (e)) and when making orders about who should pay costs (see CPR rule 44.3(5) (a)).

4.2 The court will expect the parties to have complied with this Practice Direction or any relevant pre-action protocol. The court may ask the parties to explain what steps were taken to comply prior to the start of the claim. Where there has been a failure of compliance by a party the court may ask that party to provide an explanation.'

Paragraphs 4.4 deals with examples of non-compliance and it includes:

'(3) Unreasonably refused to consider ADR' (Paragraph 8 in Part III of this Practice Direction and the Pre-Action Protocols all contain similar provisions about ADR);

All the Pre-Action Protocols do indeed require consideration of the use of ADR and where there is no applicable Pre-Action Protocol, paragraph 8 of Section III of the Practice Direction provides:

'8.1 Starting proceedings should usually be a step of last resort, and proceedings should not normally be started when a settlement is still actively being explored. Although ADR

is not compulsory, the parties should consider whether some form of ADR procedure might enable them to settle the matter without starting proceedings. The court may require evidence that the parties considered some form of ADR (see paragraph 4.4(3)).

8.2   It is not practicable in this Practice Direction to address in detail how the parties might decide to resolve a matter. However, some of the options for resolving a matter without starting proceedings are –

(1)   discussion and negotiation;
(2)   mediation (a form of negotiation with the help of an independent person or body)
(3)   early neutral evaluation (where an independent person or body, for example a lawyer or an expert in the subject, gives an opinion on the merits of a dispute); or
(4)   arbitration (where an independent person or body makes a binding decision), many types of business are members of arbitration schemes for resolving disputes with consumers.'

then:

'8.4   The parties should continue to consider the possibility of reaching a settlement at all times. This still applies after proceedings have been started, up to and during any trial or final hearing.'

So, not only may it be very much better for your client to consider ADR at the outset and throughout the proceedings, your client may well face sanctions including significant costs penalties, if this is not done.

The CPR have, thus far, stopped short of requiring parties to attempt ADR as a prerequisite to being able to commence litigation, a requirement which has been imposed in several jurisdictions, notably in Australia. The more recently drafted Family Procedure Rules (FPR) have not shown this restraint. They contain provisions very similar to those in the CPR but they go further.

Part 3 of the FPR is specifically devoted to ADR and it is headed: '*NON COURT DISPUTE RESOLUTION*'. The way it is expressed is curiously inverted but the effect is very clear. Paragraph 3.3(1) provides that:

'*(1) The court must consider, at every stage in proceedings, whether non-court dispute resolution is appropriate.*'

Part 3 goes on to require that in most Private Law family cases involving either finance or children the parties must attend a Family Mediation Information and Assessment Meeting, usually referred to as a 'MIAM' with a family mediator before they can commence proceedings.

'*3.7. An application to initiate any of the proceedings specified in Rule 3.6 must contain, or be accompanied by, a form containing, either –*

(a) a confirmation from an authorised family mediator that the prospective applicant has attended a MIAM;

(b) *a claim by the prospective applicant that one of the MIAM exemptions applies; (A list of MIAM exemptions is set out in Rule 3.8(1) below.) or*

(c) *a confirmation from an authorised* family mediator that a mediator's exemption applies. (A list of mediator's exemptions is set out in Rule 3.8(2) below.).

The proceedings specified in Rule 3.6 are:

'**3.6** *(1) The MIAM requirement applies to any application to initiate the proceedings specified in paragraph (2), unless a MIAM exemption or a mediator's exemption applies.*
  (2) The specified proceedings are –
    (a) the private law proceedings relating to children specified in Practice Direction 3A; and
    (b) the proceedings for a financial remedy specified in Practice Direction 3A.'

There then follows a very large section on MIAMs and how they are to be conducted.

The result is that if you become a professional advocate you may well be called upon to advise a client to participate in ADR. You may be required to conduct your client's case at an ADR hearing. Finally, in a family case your client may well be forced into an ADR process, albeit one in which you are unlikely to be directly involved.

CHAPTER 10

ENHANCING YOUR EMPLOYABILITY

There is no magic to achievement. It's really about hard work, choices and persistence.
Michelle Obama

1. Introduction

This chapter is intended to illustrate how you can use some of the skills contained in this book in order to enhance your prospects of obtaining a pupillage, a training contract, any other legal job, or to some extent, any other job or position.

There are, broadly, three ways in which this can be done:

1. You can use your public speaking skills in job interviews or in any other circumstance in which you have to present yourself orally.

2. You can use the research, analytical and presentational techniques set out in this book to identify and to list the skills you have acquired from this book, from your legal studies and from any other significant task you have undertaken. You will then be able both to list the skills that you have acquired and to demonstrate to a prospective employer that you have them.

3. You can apply your analytical and research skills in drafting your CV or any other written application or communication.

2. Use of Your Public Speaking Skills

Practising and developing your public speaking skills will almost certainly have improved your personal confidence and should have enabled you to be reasonably comfortable in speaking to an audience.

You will demonstrate this not just by what you say, but by the way you say it. If it is evident that you have learned to speak slowly and clearly, to talk to your audience, not at them, to think and to speak in complete sentences, to use inclusive language and to express yourself effectively using the devices of rhetoric, you are likely to be much more impressive in an interview than would otherwise be the case. It will it also be evident that you are articulate, that you think before you speak and that you consider what you say with care.

This will enhance your chances of success in any job application but, in particular, you will already have achieved a high level of competence in the use of language which is one of the most important skills required of an applicant for a pupillage or a training contract.

3. Identifying the Skills You Have Acquired

There is no universally accepted definition of the expression 'employment skills' nor of 'employability skills'. We use the expressions in the general sense of any skills which may be useful in the course of any particular employment.

The Quality Assurance Agency ('QAA') is an independent body entrusted by HM Government with the task of monitoring and advising on standards and quality in higher education. The Agency publishes guidance for employers and others on what to expect of graduates in most university subjects. These publications usually list the skills graduates are expected to have acquired under three headings:

1. Key Skills/Abilities.
2. General Transferrable Skills/Abilities.
3. Subject Specific Skills/Abilities.

Key Skills are the basic requirements of almost any job or profession:

1. Numeracy and literacy.
2. The ability to communicate both orally and in writing.
3. IT skills.
4. The ability to organise yourself to work efficiently and to do so either by yourself or as a member of a team.

Advocacy and Public Speaking

General Transferable Skills are skills which, while not of universal application, are useful in a range of activities. Skill in oratory is an example. It is of use not merely in advocacy but also in sales, politics, teaching, public relations and many other professions.

Subject Specific Skills (or Job Specific Skills) are exactly what the title says, i.e. the specific skills required for a specific job.

It may not be obvious immediately, but if you obtain a good law degree from a good university, if you read this book, learn what it attempts to teach and, as it advises, take part in mooting, mock trials and any other opportunity to practise speaking in public, you will then have acquired a significant level of skills in all three categories.

This assertion can readily be backed up by reference to the QAA publication relating to a Bachelor's Honours Degree in Law or Legal Studies which states:

'2.1 This subject benchmark statement sets out the minimum achievement which a student should demonstrate before they are awarded an honours degree in law. The vast majority of students will perform significantly better in many aspects.'

It goes on to analyse what a student is required to achieve before a degree can be awarded. Under the heading '**Subject Specific Abilities**' it lists (what follows is not a direct quotation, it is abbreviated, without, it is hoped, altering the meaning):

Knowledge:

Basic knowledge and understanding of the principal features of the legal system(s) studied.

Knowledge of a substantial range of concepts, values, principles and rules of that system and ability to explain its main legal institutions and procedures.

The study in depth and in context of some substantive areas of the legal system.

Application and Problem Solving:

Basic ability to apply knowledge to a situation of limited complexity in order to provide arguable conclusions for concrete problems (actual or hypothetical).

Sources and Research:

Basic ability to identify accurately issues which require research and to identify and retrieve up-to-date legal information using paper and electronic sources, and to use primary and secondary legal sources relevant to the topic under study.

As to **General Transferable Skills** it requires:

Basic ability to recognise and rank items and issues in terms of relevance and importance, to bring together information and materials from a variety of different sources and to produce a synthesis of relevant doctrinal and policy issues in relation to a topic.

Ability to make critical judgements on the merits of particular arguments and to present and make a reasoned choice between alternative solutions.

Autonomy and Ability to Learn:

Basic ability, with limited guidance, to act independently in planning and undertaking tasks in areas of law which they have already studied, to undertake independent research in areas of law which they have not previously studied, starting from standard legal information sources, and to reflect on their own learning and to seek and make use of feedback.

Finally, under the heading **Key Skills**, it requires:

Communication and Literacy:

Basic ability to understand and use the English language (or when appropriate Welsh) both orally and in writing.

Proficiency in relation to legal matters, to present knowledge or an argument in a way which is comprehensible to others and which is directed at their concerns, to read and discuss legal materials which are written in complex or technical language.

Numeracy, Information Technology and Teamwork:

Basic ability to use, present and evaluate information provided in numerical or statistical form in order to support an argument, to produce a word-processed essay or other text and to present such work in an appropriate form, to use the Internet, email and electronic information retrieval systems and to work in a group as an effective participant who contributes effectively to the group's task.

So an honours graduate in law who has studied and learned what this book tries to teach, will already have a significant level of employability skills. They are certainly sufficient for many jobs as a para-legal.

Analysis is important. It often discloses skills and abilities which would not otherwise be apparent. As an example, consider participation in a mooting competition.

One of the authors asked a group of students to list the skills they thought would be acquired by taking part in a mooting competition. The most common reply was *'public speaking'*. In many of the responses this was the only item on the list. But if you analyse the activities involved it becomes obvious that mooting experience provides very much more.

In order to take part effectively in a moot, you need to:

(a) Organise your working time so that you work efficiently despite competing demands on your time. (Do you prepare for the moot or complete that essay which is near its deadline?)

(**Time management** and **Work efficiency**)

(b) Identify the area of law relevant to the mooting problem and find the primary and persuasive sources of law applicable to it.

(**Analysis, Research**)

(c) Assemble the data from the sources and construct and present the argument.

(**Analysis, Deduction, Presentation**)

(d) Work on your own and as a member of a team, albeit only a small one (usually two).

(**Autonomy, Teamwork**)

The analysis need not be limited to legal matters. Most students undertake sporting or other leisure activities and these may well require the development of key or transferable skills, especially if they involve organisational responsibilities, perhaps as captain of a sporting team or secretary or treasurer of a society.

As an example, if you have taken part in the Duke of Edinburgh's Gold Award scheme and if as part of doing so you have undertaken the expedition, you have demonstrated a significant number of skills. If you list each activity and put alongside it the skill involved, the analysis becomes clear as follows:

ACTION	SKILLS REQUIRED
Select and contact others to form a team	Research, Communication Organisation
Plan the Expedition: ascertain the criteria, plan the route plan for potential problems	Research Time management Organisation Analysis Communication
Discuss the idea with instructors	Communication Analysis
Obtain the equipment required for the expedition	Research, Organisation Analysis
Carry out the expedition	Teamwork Leadership Decision-making

You will recognise from this example that no matter what task you undertake the likelihood is that you will employ and/or develop a number of skills in order to achieve success. The common misconception is that a single task only really focuses on enhancing a single skill. As you can see from the example this is just not the case. So consider all your previous achievements and experiences, analyse them and identify the skills which you have developed and used.

All too often, applicants drafting personal statements or CVs leave out any reference to their time at university other than the degree subject and classification. As a result, they fail to point out to employers attributes which might well have made the application much more attractive.

So not only should you take advantage of the opportunities offered by your university for both study and extracurricular activities, you should consider, in the light of what is required by the job description, whether to include reference to them in any job application.

When you begin your university career, it is to be expected that your CV will be rather sparse but even then, if you analyse what you have achieved thus far and the skills required to achieve it, this will give you some basis for setting out your skills and abilities.

4. Drafting Your CV

The process of drafting a CV is something of an art form. A balance must be struck between a Twitter post with only 10 or 15 words at one extreme and your autobiography at the other. If the document is too short you will not be able fully to demonstrate your suitability for the prospective post. If it is too long, there is a serious risk that no one will ever read it.

There is a vast amount of material both in paper publications and on the Internet which offers advice on how to draft a CV. This includes many websites which provide templates which they say will give your CV a professional and polished appearance.

We advise very strongly against using a template. We realise these look very flashy but they are designed with a number of applications in mind. They are too generic, they cater for a wide range of industries and trying to cram your information into formatted boxes is far from ideal. By contrast, to produce something which was obviously drafted individually shows that the candidate is sufficiently keen to obtain the post to have taken a great deal of trouble in preparing the application.

A CV should be drafted individually for each application with reference to the job requirements. These will almost invariably be set out somewhere in the document inviting applications, usually following a phrase such as *'the successful candidate will be ...'* or *'applicants should be able to ...'*. What the CV should do is to demonstrate briefly but effectively that you possess in large measure the skills they are asking for.

What is needed is a 'bespoke' CV which demonstrates that the applicant does possess the required skills by referring to the experiences in his or her life which required the exercise of those skills. This is not necessarily inconsistent with the use of a template but it is much easier to do it without one. It is far better to devise a format to suit the data than to try to force the data into a predetermined, and possibly unsuitable, format.

To adopt one of the rhetorical skills suggested in this book and to resort to metaphor, if you invited some guests to your home and offered to cook them a gourmet meal and then you served one or two courses which had obviously been bought ready-made, even if the items concerned were bought from an expensive delicatessen, you would expect the guests to be disappointed. Another analogy is that a handcrafted oak side table may lack the precise right angles and very straight edges of its laminate clad MDF equivalent but to most people it is a much more desirable object.

You should, as a matter of standard practice, keep on file in your computer the basic data which makes up your CV and you should ensure that it is always up to date but you should use the data to draft an individual CV in support of each application. Keeping the essential data up to date will enable you to do so very quickly.

Some organisations have moved to online application forms but the combination of a CV and a covering letter is still by far the most common form of application required. This is particularly the case when applying for a work experience placement in the legal field. Except for a handful of summer vacation schemes, almost all the firms, chambers, and organisations which provide such placements request a CV and covering letter. You may well be asked for these documents at relatively short notice. Having the essential core data readily to hand will help to reduce the risk of missing any potential opportunities.

There are a number of general rules and guidelines:

(1) Keep it short! A CV should not be more than two pages of A4 in length.

(2) Format. Ensure your CV is not text heavy. Don't be afraid to have some 'white space' on your page. This will make it more appealing to read.

(3) Writing style. Short and to the point. Make good use of bullet points and subheadings.

(4) Always list attainments, educational institutions attended, etc. in reverse date order, i.e. most recent first.

(5) Check the finished CV at least three times to ensure there are no typing or spelling errors, bad grammar or incorrect punctuation.

(6) Send it in good time. Employers are far less tolerant of late submissions than university tutors waiting for essays. It is very rare indeed for a late application to be considered at all.

POSTSCRIPT

'In my youth,' said his father, 'I took to the law,
And argued each case with my wife;
And the muscular strength, which it gave to my jaw,
Has lasted the rest of my life.
Lewis Carroll – 'You are Old, Father William'

Now that you have read this book, the authors hope that the objective has been achieved and you are well on the way to being confident and competent when speaking in public, that you are equipped with both a map and a compass with which to navigate your studies of the law and a satnav to guide your career as an advocate. As the builders of the campanile at Pisa discovered, if you want to build something high, you need solid foundations. We hope also that you can now use your skills to help you to attain the peaks of whatever profession you choose to enter.

The three most important rules are encapsulated in three P words:

(1)   **Prepare** everything very thoroughly.
(2)   **Peruse**. If you are to study law, read the law reports.
(3)   **Practise** your skills at every reasonable opportunity.

We wish each of our readers every success for the future.

Peroration

If proficiency in public proclamation is your aim,
Or the courtroom has been chosen as the place where
    you make hay,
You must learn the skills of rhetoric and use them just
    the same,
As Elizabeth the First or JFK.

If you're to be an advocate and enter law's great fray,
If you wish to be successful, if each jury you would
    Tame,
You must read the law report of every case along the
    Way,
And remember each authority by name.

You will need to show full knowledge of the law in
    every claim,
In every case, in every word you say,
So make thorough preparation the gravamen of your
    Game,
And practise, practise, practise, every day.

APPENDIX

SOME GREAT SPEECHES

With annotations showing the
rhetorical techniques used by the speakers

Queen Elizabeth I: Speech to her army before the arrival of the Spanish Armada, 1588

'My loving people, we[1] have been persuaded by some, that are careful of our safety, to take heed how we commit ourselves to armed multitudes, for fear of treachery; but I assure you, I do not desire to live to distrust my faithful and loving people.

Let tyrants fear; I have always so behaved myself that, under God, I have placed my chiefest strength and safeguard in the loyal hearts and good will of my subjects. And therefore I am come amongst you, as you see, at this time, not as for my recreation and disport, but being resolved, in the midst and heat of the battle, to live or die amongst you all; to lay down, for my God,

---

[1] This wording, using 'we' and 'our' in the first sentence is common to most typewritten versions of the speech. The copy of the handwritten original available on the British Library website (which can be viewed under magnification) appears to say 'I' and 'my'. If the initial uses of the plural form (which is not repeated later in the speech) are correct, they must be taken to be the Royal use of the words and therefore mean 'I' and 'my'. Nonetheless, the language used in the speech as a whole is very inclusive.

and for my kingdom, and my people, my honour and my blood, even in the dust.[2]

I know I have the body but of a weak and feeble woman; but I have the heart and stomach of a king[3], and of a king of England, too; and think foul scorn that Parma or Spain, or any prince[4] of Europe, should dare to invade the borders of my realms: to which, rather than any dishonour should grow by me, I myself will take up arms; I myself will be your general, judge, and rewarder of every one of your virtues in the field.

I know already, by your forwardness, that you have deserved rewards and crowns; and we do assure you, on the word of a prince, they shall be duly paid you.[5]

In the mean time my lieutenant general shall be in my stead, than whom never prince commanded a more noble or worthy subject; not doubting by your obedience to my general, by your concord in the camp, and by your valour in the field[6], we shall shortly have a famous victory over the enemies of my God, of my kingdom, and of my people.'[7]

---

[2] Again, very inclusive language. She expresses willingness to die among her soldiers.

[3] Contrasting phrases: 'weak body of a woman', 'heart of a king'.

[4] Rule of three 'Parma, Spain or ... Prince'.

[5] Inclusive language.

[6] Rule of three: obedience, concord and valour.

[7] Rule of three: God, kingdom and people.

Abraham Lincoln: The Gettysburg Address, 19 November 1863[8]

'Fourscore and seven years ago[9] our fathers brought forth on this continent a new nation conceived in liberty and dedicated to the proposition that all men are created equal.[10]

Now we are engaged in a great civil war, testing whether that nation, or any nation so conceived and so dedicated, can long endure.

We are met on a great battlefield of that war. We have come to dedicate a portion of that field as a final resting place for those who here gave their lives that that nation might live.[11]

It is altogether fitting and proper that we should do this. But in a larger sense we cannot dedicate, we cannot consecrate, we cannot hallow this ground.[12] The brave men, living and dead, who struggled here have consecrated it far above our poor power to add or detract.

---

[8] This is an outstanding example of 'Keep it Short'. The entire speech is only 272 words.

[9] Appropriate language – use of formal language for the 87 years since 1776 gives an air of solemnity to the opening of the speech.

[10] Quotation from the Declaration of Independence.

[11] Inclusive language: 'Our fathers', 'we are engaged', 'we are met', 'we have come'.

[12] Repeated key phrase and rule of three: 'we cannot' used three times in quick succession.

The world will little note, nor long remember what we say here, but it can never forget what they did here.[13] It is for us the living, rather, to be dedicated here to the unfinished work which they who fought here have thus far so nobly advanced.

It is rather for us to be here dedicated to the great task remaining before us – that from these honoured dead we take increased devotion to that cause for which they here gave the last full measure of devotion – that we here highly resolve that these dead shall not have died in vain – that this nation,[14] under God, shall have a new birth of freedom,[15] and that government of the people, by the people, for the people,[16] shall not perish from the earth.'

---

[13] An unintended irony. Most of the English speaking world does remember what he said. Far fewer remember the battle.

[14] Repeated key phrase 'Nation' is used five times.

[15] Metaphor: 'birth of freedom'.

[16] Rule of three: 'People' is used three times.

Susan B Anthony
Womens' Votes Campaign Speech 1873[17]

'Friends and Fellow Citizens:[18] I stand before you tonight under indictment for the alleged crime of having voted at the last presidential election, without having a lawful right to vote.

It shall be my work this evening to prove to you that in thus voting, I not only committed no crime, but, instead, simply exercised my citizen's rights, guaranteed to me and all United States citizens by the National Constitution, beyond the power of any State to deny.[19]

The preamble of the Federal Constitution[20] says:

'We, the people of the United States, in order to form a more perfect union, establish justice, insure domestic tranquillity, provide for the common defence, promote the general welfare, and secure the blessings of liberty to ourselves and our posterity, do ordain and establish this Constitution for the United States of America.'

---

[17] This speech was made several times by Susan B Anthony in 1873 when she was campaigning for women's votes after being fined for voting in the 1872 Presidential Election. It is a very interesting example for this book because not only did the speaker use several rhetorical devices, she also presented a very well argued point of law.

[18] Inclusive language.

[19] Three part speech. The Introduction.

[20] Use a quotation (and one which is also a binding authority).

It was we, the people; not we, the white male citizens; nor yet we, the male citizens; but we, the whole people, who formed the Union.[21] And we formed it, not to give the blessings of liberty, but to secure them; not to the half of ourselves and the half of our posterity, but to the whole people – women as well as men. And it is a downright mockery to talk to women of their enjoyment of the blessings of liberty while they are denied the use of the only means of securing them provided by this democratic-republican government – the ballot.[22]

For any State to make sex a qualification that must ever result in the disfranchisement of one entire half of the people is to pass a bill of attainder, or an ex post facto law, and is therefore a violation of the supreme law of the land. By it the blessings of liberty are forever withheld from women and their female posterity. To them this government has no just powers derived from the consent of the governed. To them this government is not a democracy.[23] It is not a republic. It is an odious aristocracy; a hateful oligarchy of sex; the most hateful aristocracy ever established on the face of the globe; an oligarchy of wealth, where the right govern the poor.

---

[21] Contrasting phrases.

[22] Contrasting phrases and rule of three: 'not to give the blessings, but to secure them', 'not to the half ... but to the whole' and 'Downright mockery ... enjoyment of the blessings of liberty ... denied the only means of securing them'.

[23] An impeccably presented legal argument.

An oligarchy of learning, where the educated govern the ignorant, or even an oligarchy of race, where the Saxon rules the African, might be endured; but this oligarchy of sex, which makes father, brothers, husband, sons, the oligarchs over the mother and sisters, the wife and daughters of every household – which ordains all men sovereigns, all women subjects, carries dissension, discord and rebellion into every home of the nation.[24]

Webster, Worcester and Bouvier[25] all define a citizen to be a person in the United States, entitled to vote and hold office.

The only question left to be settled now is: Are women persons?[26] And I hardly believe any of our opponents will have the hardihood to say they are not. Being persons, then, women are citizens; and no State has a right to make any law, or to enforce any old law, that shall abridge their privileges or immunities.[27]

Hence, every discrimination against women in the constitutions and laws of the several States is today null and void, precisely as in every one against Negroes.'[28]

---

[24] Repeated key phrase; 'an oligarchy'. The paragraph also contains several very strong metaphors.

[25] Rule of three.

[26] Rhetorical question.

[27] The end of the 'Main Body' of the three part speech.

[28] Conclusion of the three part speech.

Winston Churchill: 'We Shall Fight' Speech to the House of Commons, 4 June 1940

[What follows is just the last few paragraphs, not the full text of the speech which was made just after the evacuation of 338,000 allied troops from Dunkerque.]

'Turning once again, and this time more generally, to the question of invasion, I would observe that there has never been a period in all these long centuries of which we boast when an absolute guarantee against invasion, still less against serious raids, could have been given to our people.[29]

In the days of Napoleon the same wind which would have carried his transports across the Channel might have driven away the blockading fleet. There was always the chance, and it is that chance which has excited and befooled the imaginations of many continental tyrants. Many are the tales that are told.

We are assured that novel methods will be adopted, and when we see the originality of malice, the ingenuity of aggression, which our enemy displays, we may certainly prepare ourselves for every kind of novel stratagem and every kind of brutal and treacherous manoeuvre[30], I think that no idea is so outlandish that it should not be considered and viewed with a

---

[29] Single sentence of 50 words gives an air of gravity to the speech.

[30] Three uses of very strong descriptive phrases for the behaviour of the enemy: 'originality of malice', 'ingenuity of aggression' and 'brutal and treacherous manoeuvre'.

searching eye, but at the same time, I hope, with a steady eye.[31] We must never forget the solid assurances of sea power and those which belong to air power if it can be locally exercised.

I have, myself, full confidence that if all do their duty, if nothing is neglected, and if the best arrangements are made,[32] as they are being made, we shall prove ourselves once again able to defend our Island home,[33] to ride out the storm of war, and to outlive the menace of tyranny,[34] if necessary for years, if necessary alone.

At any rate, that is what we are going to try to do. That is the resolve of His Majesty's Government – every man of them. That is[35] the will of Parliament and the nation.

The British Empire and the French Republic, linked together in their cause and in their need, will defend to the death their native soil, aiding each other like good comrades[36] to the utmost of their strength.

Even though large tracts of Europe and many old and famous States have fallen or may fall into the grip

---

[31] A single sentence of 76 words.

[32] Rule of three: three consecutive clauses beginning 'if'.

[33] Inclusive language: 'we shall', 'our Island home'.

[34] Rule of three: three consecutive clauses beginning 'to'.

[35] Rule of three: three consecutive clauses beginning 'That is'.

[36] Use of simile.

of the Gestapo and all the odious apparatus[37] of Nazi rule, we shall not flag or fail.[38]

We shall go on to the end. We shall fight[39] in France. We shall fight on the seas and oceans. We shall fight with growing confidence and growing strength in the air. We shall defend our Island, whatever the cost may be. We shall fight on the beaches. We shall fight on the landing grounds. We shall fight in the fields and in the streets. We shall fight in the hills.

We shall never surrender, and even if, which I do not for a moment believe, this Island or a large part of it were subjugated and starving, then our Empire beyond the seas, armed and guarded by the British Fleet, would carry on the struggle, until, in God's good time, the New World, with all its power and might, steps forth to the rescue and the liberation of the old.'[40]

---

[37] Strong descriptive language: 'odious apparatus'.

[38] Alliteration.

[39] The Repeated key phrase for which this speech is famous: 'We shall fight'.

[40] Single sentence of 70 words.

Winston Churchill
'This Was their Finest Hour'
Speech to the House of Commons, 18 June 1940

[Again, this is not the full text of the speech, just the last few paragraphs.]

'During the first four years of the last war the Allies experienced nothing but disaster and disappointment.[41] That was our constant fear: one blow after another, terrible losses, frightful dangers. Everything miscarried.[42] And yet at the end of those four years the morale of the Allies was higher than that of the Germans, who had moved from one aggressive triumph to another, and who stood everywhere triumphant invaders of the lands into which they had broken. During that war we repeatedly asked ourselves the question: How are we going to win? and no one was able ever to answer it with much precision, until at the end, quite suddenly, quite unexpectedly, our terrible foe collapsed before us, and we were so glutted with victory[43] that in our folly we threw it away.

We do not yet know what will happen in France or whether the French resistance will be prolonged, both in France and in the French Empire overseas. The French Government will be throwing away great

---

[41] Alliteration.
[42] Rule of three: 'terrible losses, frightful dangers, everything miscarried'.
[43] Metaphor.

opportunities and casting adrift their future[44] if they do not continue the war in accordance with their Treaty obligations, from which we have not felt able to release them. The House will have read the historic declaration in which, at the desire of many Frenchmen – and of our own hearts – we have proclaimed our willingness at the darkest hour in French history to conclude a union of common citizenship in this struggle. However matters may go in France or with the French Government, or other French Governments, we[45] in this Island and in the British Empire will never lose our sense of comradeship with the French people. If we are now called upon to endure what they have been suffering, we shall emulate their courage, and if final victory rewards our toils they shall share the gains, aye, and freedom shall be restored to all. We abate nothing of our just demands; not one jot or tittle[46] do we recede. Czechs, Poles, Norwegians, Dutch, Belgians have joined their causes to our own. All these shall be restored.

What General Weygand called the Battle of France is over. I expect that the Battle of Britain is about to begin. Upon this battle depends the survival of Christian civilization. Upon it depends our own British life, and the long continuity of our institutions and our Empire.[47] The whole fury and might of the enemy must

---

[44] Metaphor.

[45] Inclusive language. Repeated use of 'we' and 'our'.

[46] Metaphor.

[47] Rule of three: 'life', 'institutions' and 'empire'.

very soon be turned on us. Hitler knows that he will have to break us in this Island or lose the war. If we can stand up to him, all Europe may be free and the life of the world may move forward into broad, sunlit uplands.[48] But if we fail, then the whole world, including the United States, including all that we have known and cared for, will sink into the abyss of a new Dark Age[49] made more sinister, and perhaps more protracted, by the lights of perverted science[50]. Let us therefore brace ourselves to our duties, and so bear ourselves that, if the British Empire and its Commonwealth last for a thousand years, men will still say, "This was their finest hour".'

---

[48] Metaphor.

[49] Metaphor.

[50] Very strong descriptive words 'perverted science'.

John F Kennedy: Inaugural Address
20 January 1961

Vice President Johnson, Mr. Speaker, Mr. Chief Justice President Eisenhower, Vice President Nixon, President Truman, reverend clergy, fellow citizens:

We observe today — [51] — not a victory of party, but a celebration of freedom — [52] — symbolizing an end, as well as a beginning — [53] — signifying renewal, as well as change. For I have sworn before you and Almighty God the same solemn oath our forebears prescribed nearly a century and three-quarters ago.

The world is very different now. For man holds in his mortal hands[54] the power to abolish all forms of human poverty and all forms of human life.[55] And yet the same revolutionary beliefs for which our forebears fought are still at issue around the globe — [56] — the belief that the rights of man come not from the generosity of the state, but from the hand of God.

We dare not forget today that we[57] are the heirs of that first revolution. Let the word go forth from this

---

[51] He paused at his point.

[52] He paused again.

[53] And again.

[54] Metaphor.

[55] Contrasting phrases.

[56] Yet another pause.

[57] Inclusive language. Repeated use of 'we'.

time and place, to friend and foe[58] alike, that the torch[59] has been passed to a new generation of Americans — born in this century, tempered by war, disciplined by a hard and bitter peace,[60] proud of our ancient heritage, and unwilling to witness or permit the slow undoing of those human rights to which this nation has always been committed, and to which we are committed today at home and around the world.

Let every nation know, whether it wishes us well or ill, that we[61] shall pay any price, bear any burden, meet any hardship, support any friend, oppose any foe, to assure the survival and the success of liberty.

This much we pledge — and more.

To those old allies whose cultural and spiritual origins we share, we[62] pledge the loyalty of faithful friends. United there is little we cannot do in a host of cooperative ventures. Divided there is little we can do — for we dare not meet a powerful challenge at odds and split asunder.

To those new states[63] whom we welcome to the ranks of the free,[64] we pledge our word that one form of colonial control shall not have passed away merely

---

[58] Alliteration.

[59] Metaphor.

[60] Double metaphor.

[61] 'We' again.

[62] And again.

[63] Contrasting phrases: 'old allies', 'new states'.

[64] Metaphor.

to be replaced by a far more iron tyranny.[65] We shall not always expect to find them supporting our[66] view. But we shall always hope to find them strongly supporting their own freedom — and to remember that, in the past, those who foolishly sought power by riding the back of the tiger ended up inside.[67]

To those people in the huts and villages of half the globe struggling to break the bonds of mass misery[68], we pledge our best efforts to help them help themselves, for whatever period is required – not because the Communists may be doing it, not because we seek their votes, but because it is right. If a free society cannot help the many who are poor, it cannot save the few who are rich.[69]

To our sister republics[70] south of our border, we offer a special pledge: to convert our good words into good deeds, in a new alliance for progress, to assist free men and free governments in casting off the chains of poverty.[71] But this peaceful revolution of hope cannot become the prey of hostile powers.[72] Let all our neighbours know that we shall join with them to oppose aggression or subversion anywhere in the

---

[65] Metaphor.

[66] Six consecutive uses of 'we' or 'our'.

[67] Metaphor.

[68] Metaphor.

[69] Contrasting phrases.

[70] Metaphor.

[71] Metaphor.

[72] Double metaphor.

Americas. And let every other power know that this hemisphere intends to remain the master of its own house.[73]

To that world assembly of sovereign states, the United Nations, our last best hope in an age where the instruments of war have far outpaced the instruments of peace,[74] we renew our pledge of support — to prevent it from becoming merely a forum for invective, to strengthen its shield of the new and the weak,[75] and to enlarge the area in which its writ may run.

Finally, to those nations who would make themselves our adversary, we offer not a pledge but a request: that both sides begin anew the quest for peace, before the dark powers of destruction[76] unleashed by science engulf all humanity in planned or accidental self-destruction.

We dare not tempt them with weakness. For only when our arms are sufficient beyond doubt can we be certain beyond doubt[77] that they will never be employed.

But neither can two great and powerful groups of nations take comfort from our present course — both sides overburdened by the cost of modern weapons, both rightly alarmed by the steady spread of the deadly

---

[73] Metaphor.

[74] Contrasting phrases.

[75] Metaphor.

[76] Metaphor.

[77] Repeat phrase: 'Beyond doubt'.

atom, yet both racing to alter that uncertain balance of terror that stays the hand of mankind's final war.[78]

So let us begin anew — remembering on both sides that civility is not a sign of weakness, and sincerity is always subject to proof. Let us never negotiate out of fear, but let us never fear to negotiate.[79]

Let both sides explore what problems unite us instead of belabouring those problems which divide us.[80] Let both sides, for the first time, formulate serious and precise proposals for the inspection and control of arms, and bring the absolute power to destroy other nations under the absolute control of all nations.[81]

Let both sides seek to invoke the wonders of science instead of its terrors.[82] Together let us explore the stars, conquer the deserts, eradicate disease, tap the ocean depths, and encourage the arts and commerce. Let both sides[83] unite to heed, in all corners of the earth, the command of Isaiah — to 'undo the heavy burdens, and let the oppressed go free.'[84]

And, if a beachhead of cooperation may push back the jungle of suspicion,[85] let both sides join in creating a new endeavour —[86]— not a new balance of power,

---

[78] Triple metaphor.

[79] Antimetabole.

[80] Contrasting phrases.

[81] Repeat use of 'absolute'.

[82] Contrasting phrases.

[83] Repeat key phrase: 'Let both sides' used four times.

[84] Quotation. Isaiah 58:6.

[85] Double metaphor.

[86] Double metaphor and a significant pause.

but a new world of law — [87] — where the strong are just, and the weak secure, and the peace preserved.

All this will not be finished in the first one hundred days. Nor will it be finished in the first one thousand days; nor in the life of this Administration; nor even perhaps in our lifetime on this planet. But let us begin.

In your hands, my fellow citizens,[88] more than mine, will rest the final success or failure of our course. Since this country was founded, each generation of Americans has been summoned to give testimony to its national loyalty. The graves of young Americans who answered the call to service surround the globe.

Now the trumpet summons us again,[89] not as a call to bear arms, though arms we need, not as a call to battle, though embattled we are, but a call[90] to bear the burden of a long twilight struggle, year in and year out, "rejoicing in hope; patient in tribulation", a struggle against the common enemies of man: tyranny, poverty, disease, and war itself.

Can we forge against these enemies a grand and global alliance, North and South, East and West, that can assure a more fruitful life for all mankind? Will you join in that historic effort?[91]

In the long history of the world, only a few generations have been granted the role of defending

---

[87] Double metaphor and a significant pause.

[88] Inclusive language.

[89] Metaphor.

[90] Repeat key phrase: 'a call' used three times.

[91] Two successive rhetorical questions.

freedom in its hour of maximum danger. I do not shrink from this responsibility — I welcome it. I do not believe that any of us would exchange places with any other people or any other generation. The energy, the faith, the devotion which we bring to this endeavour will light our country and all who serve it. And the glow from that fire can truly light the world.[92]

And so, my fellow Americans, ask not what your country can do for you; ask what you can do for your country.[93]

My fellow citizens of the world, ask not what America will do for you, but what together we can do for the freedom of man.[94]

Finally, whether you are citizens of America or citizens of the world, ask[95] of us here the same high standards of strength and sacrifice which we ask of you. With a good conscience our only sure reward, with history the final judge of our deeds,[96] let us go forth to lead the land we love, asking His blessing and His help, but knowing that here on earth God's work must truly be our own.'

---

[92] Double metaphor.

[93] The antimetabole for which this speech is best known.

[94] Antimetabole.

[95] Repeated use of 'ask'.

[96] Metaphor.

Some Great Speeches

John F Kennedy
'Ich Bin Ein Berliner'
Speech to a mass audience in Berlin, 26 June 1963

'I am proud to come to this city as the guest of your distinguished Mayor, who has symbolised throughout the world the fighting spirit of West Berlin.[97]

And I am proud[98] to visit the Federal Republic with your distinguished Chancellor who for so many years has committed Germany to democracy and freedom and progress,[99] and to come here in the company of my fellow American, General Clay, who has been in this city during its great moments of crisis and will come again if ever needed.

Two thousand years ago the proudest boast was *"Civis Romanus Sum"*. Today, in the world of freedom, the proudest boast is *"Ich bin ein Berliner"*.[100]

I appreciate my interpreter translating my German.[101]

There are many people in the world who really don't understand, or say they don't, what is the great

---

[97] Opening sentence with impact 'I am proud to come'.

[98] Repeated key phrase 'I am proud' used again.

[99] Rule of three: 'democracy, freedom and progress'.

[100] Use of the language of the audience.

[101] Use a joke. He implies that his German requires translation to a German audience. The translator had corrected the sentence by repeating it without the 'ein'. With it, the phrase means 'I am a doughnut.' Despite the slip it is obvious from the reaction of the audience that the use of their own language was extremely effective.

issue between the free world and the Communist world. Let them come to Berlin.[102]

There are some who say that Communism is the way of the future. Let them come to Berlin.

And there are some who say in Europe and elsewhere we can work with the Communists. Let them come to Berlin.

And there are even a few who say that it is true that Communism is an evil system, but it permits us to make economic progress. Lass' sie nach Berlin kommen. Let them come to Berlin.[103]

Freedom has many difficulties and democracy is not perfect, but we have never had to put a wall up to keep our people in, to prevent them from leaving us.

I want to say, on behalf of my countrymen, who live many miles away on the other side of the Atlantic, who are far distant from you, that they take the greatest pride that they have been able to share with you,[104] even from a distance, the story of the last 18 years.

I know of no town, no city, that has been besieged for 18 years that still lives with the vitality and the force, and the hope and the determination of the city of West Berlin.

While the wall is the most obvious and vivid demonstration of the failures of the Communist

---

[102] The first use of the Repeated key phrase 'let them come to Berlin' which occurs four times.

[103] Repeated key phrase also spoken in German.

[104] Inclusive language.

system, for all the world to see, we[105] take no satisfaction in it, for it is, as your mayor has said, an offense not only against history but an offense against humanity, separating families, dividing husbands and wives and brothers and sisters, and dividing a people who wish to be joined together.

What is true of this city is true of Germany – real, lasting peace in Europe can never be assured as long as one German out of four is denied the elementary right of free men, and that is to make a free choice.

In 18 years of peace and good faith, this generation of Germans has earned the right to be free, including the right to unite their families and their nation in lasting peace, with good will to all people.

You live in a defended island of freedom, but your life is part of the main.

So let me ask you as I close, to lift your eyes beyond the dangers of today, to the hopes of tomorrow, beyond the freedom merely of this city of Berlin, or your country of Germany, to the advance of freedom everywhere, beyond the wall to the day of peace with justice, beyond yourselves and ourselves to all mankind.

Freedom is indivisible, and when one man is enslaved, all are not free.

When all are free, then we can look forward to that day when this city will be joined as one and this country and this great continent of Europe in a peaceful and hopeful globe.

---

[105] Inclusive language.

When that day finally comes, as it will, the people of West Berlin can take sober satisfaction in the fact that they were in the front lines for almost two decades.

All free men, wherever they may live, are citizens of Berlin, and, therefore, as a free man, I take pride in the words "Ich bin ein Berliner".'

Robert F Kennedy
Speech at Indianapolis announcing the death of Martin Luther King, 4 April 1968[106]

'Ladies and Gentlemen – I'm only going to talk to you just for a minute or so this evening.[107]

Because ... I have some very sad news for all of you, and I think sad news for all of our fellow citizens, and people who love peace all over the world, and that is that Martin Luther King was shot and was killed tonight in Memphis, Tennessee.

Martin Luther King dedicated his life to love and to justice between fellow human beings. He died in the cause of that effort. In this difficult day, in this difficult time for the United States, it's perhaps well to ask what kind of a nation we are and what direction we want to move in.

For those of you who are black, considering the evidence evidently is that they were white people who

---

[106] The most striking feature of this speech is RFK's masterful use of pauses. This is not evident from the text. It is essential to listen to a recording. It is readily available online.

[107] The speech uses the three part structure. The first three paragraphs are the introduction in which he explains why he wants to speak. Then follows the main body of the speech in which RFK pays tribute to Martin Luther King and urges his audience not to respond to the murder by resorting to hatred or violence. The conclusion is in the last four paragraphs in which he repeats and summarises this message.

were responsible, you can be filled with bitterness, and with hatred, and a desire for revenge.[108]

We can move in that direction as a country, in greater polarization, black people amongst blacks, and white amongst whites, filled with hatred toward one another.

Or we can make an effort, as Martin Luther King did, to understand and to comprehend, and replace that violence, that stain of bloodshed that has spread across our land, with an effort to understand, compassion and love.

For those of you who are black and are tempted to be filled with hatred and mistrust of the injustice of such an act, against all white people, I would only say that I can also feel in my own heart the same kind of feeling. I had a member of my family killed, but he was killed by a white man.[109]

But we have to make an effort in the United States, we have to make an effort to understand, to get beyond these rather difficult times.

My favourite poet was Aeschylus. He once wrote: 'Even in our sleep, pain which cannot forget falls drop by drop upon the heart, until, in our own despair, against our will, comes wisdom through the awful grace of God.'[110]

---

[108] Rule of three: 'bitterness', 'hatred' and 'revenge'.

[109] Superb example of inclusive language with a very high emotional content.

[110] Quotation from Aeschylus' play 'Agamemnon'.

What we need in the United States is not division; what we need in the United States is not hatred; what we need in the United States[111] is not violence and lawlessness, but is love and wisdom, and compassion toward one another, and a feeling of justice toward those who still suffer within our country, whether they be white or whether they be black.

So I ask you tonight to return home, to say a prayer for the family of Martin Luther King, yes that's true, but more importantly to say a prayer for our own country,[112] which all of us love, a prayer for understanding and that compassion of which I spoke. We can do well in this country. We will have difficult times. We've had difficult times in the past. And we will have difficult times in the future. It is not the end of violence; it is not the end of lawlessness; and it's not the end of disorder.

But the vast majority of white people and the vast majority of black people in this country want to live together, want to improve the quality of our life,[113] and want justice for all human beings that abide in our land.

---

[111] Repeated key phrase: 'What we need in the United States' – used three times.

[112] Use of inclusive language: 'our own country, which all of us love' followed by four consecutive sentences using 'we'.

[113] Inclusive language 'our life' followed by 'all human beings' and the final two paragraphs beginning 'let us'.

Let us dedicate ourselves to what the Greeks wrote so many years ago: 'to tame the savageness of man and make gentle the life of this world'.[114]

Let us dedicate ourselves to that, and say a prayer for our country and for our people. Thank you very much.'[115]

---

[114] Quotation. RFK does not say so but this quotation is also from Aeschylus.

[115] Notice also that despite being delivered without a single look at the note in the speaker's hand, the speech has not one unfinished sentence.

COPYRIGHT ACKNOWLEDGEMENTS

In the United States any work prepared by an officer or employee of the United States Government as part of that person's official duties is in the public domain under the terms of Title 17, Chapter 1, and Section 105 of the United States Code. As a result, this covers the speeches by John F Kennedy and Robert F Kennedy as one was the President and the other was Senator for New York.

The speeches by Winston Churchill used in this book were all made to the House of Commons. As such any copyright is owned by Parliament and there is a general licence to use such material called the Open Parliament Licence. Therefore, this publication contains Parliamentary information licensed under the Open Parliament Licence v3.0 and further information on its use is available at:

http://www.parliament.uk/site-information/copyright/open-parliament-licence

As to the sections from the professional conduct rules reproduced in Chapter 9, all three publishing bodies were contacted by the authors before the publication of this volume and they confirmed that there was no restriction on their reproduction.

The QAA publications quoted or paraphrased in Chapter 10 are in the public domain.

All other quotations in this book are attributed and are either out of copyright, or are too short to infringe copyright, or both.